MERCY MATTERS

OPENING YOURSELF TO THE LIFE-CHANGING GIFT

MATHEW N. SCHMALZ

Our Sunday Visitor

www.osv.com
Our Sunday Visitor Publishing Division
Our Sunday Visitor, Inc.
Huntington, Indiana 46750

Our Sunday Visitor Publishing Division
Our Sunday Visitor, Inc.
200 Noll Plaza
Huntington, IN 46750
1-800-348-2440

ISBN: 978-1-61278-996-5 (Inventory No. T1746)
eISBN: 978-1-61278-998-9
LCCN: 2016935176

Cover design: Lindsey Riesen
Cover art: Veer
Interior design: Dianne Nelson

PRINTED IN THE UNITED STATES OF AMERICA

For Dolores T. Schmalz,
my merciful mom

*Let us then with confidence draw near
to the throne of grace, that we may
receive mercy and find grace
to help in time of need.*

– Hebrews 4:16

CONTENTS

ACKNOWLEDGMENTS

This book is about opening ourselves to mercy, to love that responds to human need in an unexpected or unmerited way. This book is itself the result of many mercies shown to me by many people over the course of my life. While some of these people do appear in the following pages, many do not, and so I would like to acknowledge them here.

For love: My wife and daughters. They do appear in the book, although under pseudonyms of their own choosing. Our dog, Harold, has chosen his real name.

For editorial advice: Cindy Cavnar and Bill Roorbach.

For inspiration: Catherine Duclos, Mary Johnson, Joanne Pierce, and Donna Steinmetz.

For friendship: Peter Gottschalk, Keith Harmon, Father Warren Hicks, Jack Horky, Thomas Landy, and Malik Neal.

For mercies shared: David Robert Campbell, Elin Cohen, Anita Houck, Rebecca Krier, Vaughn Kurtz, Janice Lloyd, Kevin Meinert, Nestor Santana, Julia Schmalz, Hema Sharma, Kevin Walsh, and Kimberlee Wyche.

And for merciful memories: Albert Duclos, Betty Hubsch, Marzena Ladiejewska, Kim McElaney, Constance McKenna, Stephen Schmalz, Johnny T. K, and Theodore and Irene Tourangeau.

I would also like to express my gratitude to two journalist editors who have provided me encouragement and opportunity, and also gave me permission to draw upon pieces previously published online: Teresa Hanaflin of Crux (www.cruxnow.com) and Corrie Mitchell of On Faith (www.faithstreet.com/onfaith). Citations of the relevant articles may be found in the Endnotes.

INTRODUCTION

Mercy Matters

On April 11, 2015, Pope Francis proclaimed an extraordinary Jubilee of Mercy, to begin with the solemnity of the Immaculate Conception on December 8, 2015, and concluding with the feast of Christ the King, November 20, 2016.[1] There have only been three extraordinary Jubilee years in the history of the Church, the last one called by St. John Paul II in 1983 to commemorate 1,950 years since the birth of Jesus.[2] When he opened the special Holy Door in St. Peter's in Rome to inaugurate the Year of Mercy, Pope Francis remarked, "To enter through the Holy Door means to rediscover the deepness of the mercy of the Father, who welcomes all and goes out to meet everyone personally."[3] This personal relationship that God offers us is based upon a love that reaches out to us in our weakness and vulnerability. "How much wrong we do to God and his grace," Pope Francis said as he began the Jubilee, "when we speak of sins being punished by his judgment before we speak of their being forgiven by his mercy."[4]

***

Pope Francis offers extended reflections on mercy in *Misericordiae Vultus*, the Bull of Indiction proclaiming the extraordinary Jubilee Year.[5] "Jesus Christ is the face of God's mercy," it begins.[6] Mercy is what connects human beings and God, "opening our hearts to the hope of being loved forever despite our sinfulness."[7]

Misericordiae Vultus surveys how mercy is discussed in Scripture. The "Great Hallel," Psalm 136, speaks of God's mercy "enduring forever," and Jesus prayed this psalm when He and disciples went to the Mount of Olives.[8] Throughout the Gospels, Jesus responds with mercy: He healed the sick; He fed the crowds who came to see Him; He called the tax collector and sinner,

Matthew, to be one of His disciples.[9] Jesus also spoke of mercy through parables, such as the story of the "ruthless servant" who has his own substantial debt forgiven but then refuses to forgive the debt of another servant who only owed him a few cents.[10] In commenting that the first servant was put in jail by his master for this refusal, Pope Francis observes that mercy is the criterion by which the Father knows "who his true children are."[11]

Pope Francis wants us to know that God's mercy, expressed through Jesus Christ, is not abstract, but concrete. It is "visceral."[12] And it is in the life of the Church that mercy finds tangible expression. There are the sacraments: Jesus offers forgiveness in the Sacrament of Reconciliation; He offers us His very body and blood in the Eucharist. The Church recognizes and promotes corporal works of mercy: feeding the hungry, giving drink to the thirsty, clothing the naked, welcoming the stranger, healing the sick, visiting the imprisoned, and burying the dead.[13] There are also spiritual works of mercy: counseling the doubtful, instructing the ignorant, admonishing sinners, comforting the afflicted, forgiving offenses, bearing patiently those who do us ill, and praying for the living and the dead.[14]

Beyond such formalized expressions, Pope Francis wants the Church to become an "oasis of mercy" for all, by eschewing the legalism that can so often characterize our discussions of the relationship between mercy and justice.[15] In Scripture, Pope Francis reminds us, justice is primarily conceived as "the faithful abandonment of oneself to God's will."[16] Jesus abandoned himself to the will of God, His Father, and reminded us, "Go and learn what this means: 'I desire mercy, and not sacrifice.'"[17]

All of us are called to be "instruments of mercy" because we all have been shown mercy by God.[18]

What emerges in *Misericordiae Vultus* is a discussion of mercy that begins with the conventional connection between mercy and sin: that God loves sinners is in itself mercy. But *Misericor-*

diae Vultus also extends our understanding of mercy to include reaching out to others in their distress, particularly those whom society has marginalized. Mercy responds not just to human sin, but also to human need. Accordingly, to understand mercy is to see it at work throughout the complexity of human life. In proclaiming the extraordinary Jubilee of Mercy, Pope Francis is asking us to open ourselves to the diverse and varied experiences and expressions of mercy that touch all of us as human beings, in our relationship with God, and in our relationships with one another.

***

This book, *Mercy Matters: Opening Yourself to the Life-Changing Gift,* attempts to respond to Pope Francis' call for us to appreciate the importance of mercy as a central theme in God's love for us and in the life of the Church. An academic approach to understanding mercy would be careful to delineate precisely what mercy is not. But the approach taken here is different: it is designed to connect the experience and expression of mercy to other experiences and expressions of love and broaden our understanding of mercy's life-changing possibilities.

Mercy is God's loving response to sinners; and mercy is our loving response to others—and to ourselves—in circumstances of need. To this I would add that mercy, as an experience of love, has an unexpected quality—something unforeseen or unanticipated. We talk about mercy when we feel or offer forgiveness, when we find or give help and assistance, but we also speak about "mercy" when we are surprised by good deeds that catch us unawares and transform our lives. For the purpose of our discussion, mercy is love that responds to human need in an unexpected or unmerited way. Opening ourselves to the many ways mercy can touch and change us is the goal of this book.

Mercy Matters is divided into three overall sections: Mercy and Self, Mercy and Others, and Mercy and God.

"Mercy and Self," the first part, considers what it means to personally experience mercy. Chapter One speaks of the mercy of grace that can radically transform a person's life. Chapter Two addresses how mercy can lead to reconciliation in the long-term aftermath of bullying. Chapter Three argues for "letting go" as a mercy when caught in a seemingly intractable dispute with a loved one. Chapter Four examines what it means to be merciful and compassionate to yourself in a way that involves others.

"Mercy and Others," the second part, considers how mercy connects us to one another. Chapter Five examines how mercy to others depends on freedom: both the freedom to give and the freedom to receive. Chapter Six considers how mercy relates to human dignity, particularly the dignity of those whom society stigmatizes. Chapter Seven reflects on the mercy of kindness in an unlikely friendship, and how kindness as mercy relates to fear and vulnerability. Chapter Eight considers how speaking the truth can be a mercy, even though it may seem to have harsh and dreadful consequences.

"Mercy and God," the third and final part, considers how God's mercy can be understood. Chapter Nine considers mercy as forgiveness through a discussion of the Boston bombing and its aftermath. Chapter Ten looks at the question of where God's mercy can be found in the context of human suffering. Chapter Eleven reflects on what makes a death merciful beyond avoiding pain and suffering. Chapter Twelve concludes the volume by considering what mercy means when it comes to choosing life and dealing with a secret that could radically change the lives of others that we haven't met.

In each and every chapter, I have drawn on my own personal experiences. The intent behind sharing my personal experiences is not to present them as somehow special or exemplary. Instead, my hope is that by sharing my own stories and experiences of mercy, others will be encouraged and empowered to share their own stories and experiences as well. *Mercy Matters* is structured to facilitate conversation and reflection. The stories are meant to provide a concrete context for considering how complex and sometimes confusing questions of mercy arise within our own lives and in the lives of others.

In presenting the stories in the way I have, I have tried to be honest about my own views but open-ended in framing discussion. Readers should feel free to disagree with how I have interpreted the issues that I have shared and put forward. *Mercy Matters* is not a textbook that defines what mercy is or should be. Instead, it is an invitation to reflect and discern the many ways God's mercy can be made manifest for all of us.

***

Mercy Matters is a work of creative nonfiction. As nonfiction, all the experiences mentioned are "real"—they actually happened. The persons mentioned are also real—there are no composite or invented characters. I have, however, extensively used pseudonyms and a list of specific pseudonyms used in each chapter can be found at the end of the book. I have also taken care to preserve privacy by being deliberately vague about locations and potentially identifying details of certain persons: this is particularly the case in Chapters Two, Five, Seven, Eight, Nine, and Twelve.

The creative aspect of the book is reflected in how I have streamlined and simplified the narrative so that the chapters flow more smoothly. For example, a full account of my high school reunion in Chapter Two would necessarily include a discussion of how I arrived with the high school friends who invited me—but I do not mention them or that aspect of the evening so that I can keep the focus on my meeting with Zach. In Chapter Five, I have not delved into the complex back story of the attack against Ghura Paul, though I do discuss it in my academic publications about him. In Chapter Eight, as I mention briefly, I certainly was not the only person working at "Graced Opportunities," but I have only discussed "Father Ed" since he figured so strongly into my relationship with "Ricky."

Also, to enhance narrative flow, I include dialogue in most of the chapters. While I do have a very good memory for words, I will not claim that I am remembering each and every exchange verbatim. The fallibility of memory is a strong theme in Chapter Three, and that should serve as a necessary reminder that, while I have made every effort to be accurate, my memory does have its blind spots, gaps, and, most probably, unintentional imaginings. Such failings are inevitable, and so I thank everyone who reads this book for showing me mercy by allowing me to share something of myself in and through my own limitations.

PART ONE

MERCY AND SELF

Chapter One

Mercy and Grace

Stories of sobriety—like stories of conversion—are all different, but they're all the same. They're stories of mercy.

I looked at the blue sweater—looked at it intensely. It was balled up on the orange throw that just barely covered the couch.

A blue, crew-neck sweater.

I couldn't remember anything about it: how it got there, who it belonged to.

I couldn't remember much about the party either—I had a vision of me welcoming some people at the door, and putting some wine coolers in the fridge, but that was it. Now my apartment was littered with bottles.

What did I say? What did I do?

I could have done something terrible; I must have done something terrible.

That was February 19, 1993, Chicago, Illinois.

***

Several months earlier, and it was a normal Friday for me.

I was a graduate student at the Divinity School of the University of Chicago. I was about to go to a lecture and reception. I don't remember what the lecture was supposed to be about—it could have been anything from the "Religious Symbolism of Automobiles" to "The Theology of Zoos." The content wasn't important—but attendance was. In fact, showing up for lectures and receptions was the surest way to success as a graduate student: it meant being seen and recognized.

I'd wear black jeans and polished black loafers, along with a black sweater over a white turtleneck, a kind of personal uniform that I thought would make me stand out in a serious, intellectual kind of way. I liked the feeling of the tight elastic collar; I liked the look of the white emerging from that buildup of black.

I probably shaved multiple times to make sure I looked neat and tried different kinds of after-shave and cologne. Whatever the reason, I managed to get going late—very late. I missed the lecture completely and made it to the reception only after it was well underway. The room had vaulted ceilings and rich wood paneling lining the walls, cavernous and claustrophobic at the same time.

I headed straight for the wine.

It had been set out in plastic jugs—one for red, one for white. There were cheeses too: brie and Swiss cut in wedges, white and yellow cheddar sliced in neat squares, toothpicks with red cellophane bows and ruffles—the napkins had the university seal of a phoenix rising from the ashes.

Gulping wine, I prepared for questions. What authors have you read? (I just finished a collection of essays by the Jesuit theologian Karl Rahner.) What grants have you applied for? (I'm working on a Fulbright.) Have you published anything yet? (Yes, a book review on the *Guru in Indian Catholicism*.) What's your dissertation about? (The interrelationship between Hinduism and Catholicism.) What languages can you speak? (Hindi and Urdu.)

I really hoped I would hear that last question—I could talk about the two years I'd spent in India and Pakistan as a student.

Looking around, I saw a lot of unfamiliar faces. I used to know people at the Divinity School, but most had left—or had been asked to leave. Aditya, my roommate for two years, was still in the program, but had gone to India for the year to do his doctoral research. My classmate Stan was at the reception, though, looking like a rock star in his suede boots and brown leather jacket—an outfit that worked well with his long blonde hair. Smart and socially adept, he may have nodded to me, but I didn't want to piggyback on his chitchat.

Then there was Wendy, my adviser, who was an internationally known scholar of Hindu mythology. She was angry with me because I'd screwed up preparing the index of her latest book—I got drunk and left the index, partially done, in a bag by the door of her condo, past the publisher's deadline. Wendy was easy to identify wearing her black dress and leggings with her red cowboy boots—she was talking to students on the other side of the room under a stern portrait of some sort of academic dignitary. Wendy was the forgiving type, but I wondered whether I should apologize or hide.

I kept gulping wine—glass after glass after glass—it was sickly sweet, warm, and definitely not as strong as I needed.

I left without having said a word to anyone, not even goodbye.

***

I walked through the shadows of spires and gargoyles on the enclosed campus lawns. Fluorescent blue lights glowed and flickered, signaling where emergency call boxes stood guard. Where the call boxes ended the South Side of Chicago began.

I made my way back to my apartment. I had recently moved beyond university-owned housing, uncharted territory for graduate students like me, a nice, one-bedroom setup. I paid a little extra out of my scholarship money to see a sliver of Lake Michigan and the distant lights of the Hancock Building so that I wouldn't feel so confined by my graduate-school world.

After the last set of call boxes I ducked under a bridge for the commuter rail line. I noticed a man sitting on the curb on the block in front of me. He was wearing a knit cap—that's all my memory shows me now, except that he was African-American. I vowed right then and there that I wasn't going to be the typical white university student who'd look away. And I wasn't going to turn around and run back to the emergency call boxes.

I went ahead.

The man looked up at me; I looked down at him.

"Hey, can you help me out? My car broke down."

I smiled—I must have smiled. I was prepared. I said: "I know you really want a drink. I'll give you some money, but we have to drink together."

That's what I said—it was matter-of-fact and to the point.

It also was staged.

I had been rehearsing the line ever since I had managed a homeless shelter a year before graduate school. I felt important with the homeless; I was bigger in their world, almost like Superman: a normal person on his home planet but able to leap tall buildings on the otherwise alien Earth.

Besides, I was buying the booze—I knew the homeless usually don't reject that kind of mercy. My newfound friend and I walked deep into the South Side, where bookstores gave way to row homes and flats. We ended up at a liquor store with a long line—a security guard let in a couple of customers at a time. Nods, quick handshakes, and a "Hey, brother," told me that my companion was a regular.

I asked what people wanted to drink: "Whiskey!" "Rum!" "Beer!" came in rapid sequence. But looking in my pocket, I discovered that I had less cash than I thought.

"It's going to be Thunderbird," my companion said as he saw my rumpled dollar bills.

I knew about Thunderbird—the cheapest wine there was, the kind that hadn't even been introduced to a real grape.

"We need Kool-Aid," someone else added. "It'll take away the bite."

But where were we going find that? No problem: first liquor store I'd ever seen that displayed Kool-Aid packages on the counter by the cash register—you could pick them up easily when you got your fifth of Thunderbird handed to you.

We got our supplies and about five of us walked into the night together. We put the Kool-Aid in the Thunderbird, and watched it swirl and dissolve. We passed it around, mouth to mouth—I thought it bad form to wipe down the bottle before taking a swig.

Our "church" was an empty lot with a chain-link fence and our "sacrament" tasted like cherries and oranges more than grapes. Maybe it wasn't Communion, but it was *a communion*, I was sure of that—even when we started walking down the street together and I lost track of the group and had to hail a cab to get back to my apartment.

The next day, I realized that alcohol wasn't exactly the universal solvent that could dissolve distinctions of race and class—after all, I woke up in a bed, with a blanket, and there was a roof over my head, even as terrible as I felt. But maybe, I thought, just maybe I had performed an act of mercy, beyond simply buying the booze.

I had shown the homeless that I cared, that I was willing to share.

It was the mercy that mattered—not the uncomfortable fact that I couldn't remember anyone's name.

***

I wasn't the type attracted to the Polynesian novelty drinks, not at Ciral's House of Tiki, not anyplace else, but I knew the House of Tiki was there for me. I never had a zombie—with its seven kinds of liquor—and didn't feel the urge to stick my face into a flaming Scorpion bowl. I kept to Jack Daniels and chasers of Miller Draft—plunking down enough scholarship cash on the bar to keep the drinks coming.

When I loosened up, I'd even talk to the barman.

I think the barman and Ciral were actually the same person—but I never asked. In any case, it was the same barman every time I went in. He wore a floral Hawaiian shirt. His beard and mustache were well trimmed, and his brown-black hair was slicked back, curling midway down his neck.

One night, I asked whether it was true that Mayor Harold Washington used to stop by for a drink after hours. No such thing ever happened, the barman said. Another night, I tried laying the groundwork for an extended discussion:

"Wasn't this the setting for a shootout filmed for the movie *The Package*? Gene Hackman, right?"

I thought of the spiky blowfish lamps exploding with gunshots and the air thick with flying bamboo splinters and spinning drink coasters.

"No," the barman said, "we only appeared for a couple of minutes in the film."

I quickly drained my beer glass and left.

But I would be back soon enough.

The best thing about the House of Tiki was that it had beer to go, and it was open till four in the morning. The beer would keep me going until five, which was when I started to feel hungry. I liked frying up steak and eggs at dawn's light, even though I'd have to first wipe down the plates smeared with the mold growing in my kitchen sink.

I wasn't exactly born with a silver spoon in my mouth—more like a book in my hand. I was an adopted child, christened to be an academic. The one thing I knew about my time in the orphanage attached to a Catholic home for unwed mothers is that the Sisters of Providence insisted that I be put into a family with a professor: evidently, my birth mother was particularly bright, and the sisters assumed that her intellect had been passed down to me. Although this meant that I had to wait longer to be adopted, it was intended as a mercy: even if I didn't have a God-given birth family to take care of me, I would still find my God-given abilities nurtured.

And sure enough, here I was in graduate school.

But I didn't cook high-end fusion cuisine; I didn't frequent wine tastings; I didn't go to French film festivals. I ate breakfast like a farmer, like a truck driver. At night, I went to dive bars like the House of Tiki and favored Everyman actors like Gene Hackman.

I had a double life, and the flip side of my bookish coin was rougher and grittier than my classmates and advisers could imagine when they saw me in those shiny black loafers. The homeless were a relief from all that graduate-school posturing and posing.

Maybe, I realized, the homeless were the ones who sensed where I was coming from.

Maybe they were the ones who showed *me* the mercy, not the other way around.

***

A couple weeks after drinking with the homeless, I made my usual visit to the all-night grocery store for my breakfast routine. I got London broil, a dozen eggs, a brick of American cheese, and put it all in a basket. I felt good—it was the kind of drunk when I didn't feel quite drunk, just calm and collected. It was a surprise when I saw a security guard shadowing me. But no matter—like any normal customer, I engaged in some polite conversation with the woman at the cash register.

I tasted the stale beer and whiskey on my breath. My tongue was thick and my voice loud.

The woman at the cash register smiled and nodded.

But she wasn't smiling and nodding to me—she was smiling and nodding to the security guard. They both wanted to make sure that I was going on my way.

Remembering that, I never went back.

Over the next month, I also got the sense that the barman at the House of Tiki wanted me on my way as well, probably fearing another awkward attempt at conversation involving half-remembered details and made-up facts.

One night, I nodded off between my whiskey and beer, and the barman loudly snapped his fingers next to my ear. It woke me up like a fire alarm, and I left whatever cash was on the bar and staggered out.

It took me a couple of weeks to get up the courage to go back to the House of Tiki for an early-morning beer run. I had been drinking alone, heating up my VCR by going through a stack of horror films and psychological thrillers. I had finished off two six packs of Colt 45 tallboys and was ready for more. The walk to the House of Tiki was uneventful, and I was looking forward to the comforting coolness of beer cans under my arm.

I entered the House of Tiki just as I had many times before—after 2:00 a.m., it was the only bar open, and it was packed.

I went up to the barman and asked for a six of Miller to go.

"Can I see your ID?" he asked.

This hadn't happened before.

I handed over my Massachusetts driver's license—I was twenty-eight years old but looked more like eighteen. That had to be the reason.

"What's the name on the ID?"

I paused. I panicked.

"I don't know," I blurted. I couldn't think.

The barman shook his head slightly as he pushed my driver's license back to me over the bar.

Stumbling home, I realized my drinking options were becoming limited. "You're becoming a shut-in," I told myself, careful not to fall or walk into something.

I probably strung together a couple other sentences as well. "Mathew"—I'd always call myself Mathew—"Mathew, the fundamental problem is that everyone around us is such a lightweight." I'm sure I focused on Peter—a new friend, a great guy, someone to speak Hindi to and watch Star Trek with. But he didn't drink at all.

As I got closer to home, I had a moment of inspiration: change the context, stop all the sneaking around! Have a party!

It took over a week, but I worked purposefully.

I planned and I drank. I invited people and I drank. I cleaned and I drank. I was ready and I drank.

And the party happened.

That was February 18, 1993.

***

Back to the morning after. Trudging into the living room, I managed to find a corner of the carpet that wasn't soaked with something. I sat, right on the floor, opened my address book, and started dialing the phone. I was going to ask about the blue sweater—that would be pretext enough for a call. But I really wanted to know what I might have done at the party, any clue at all to begin to create a memory of that night.

I called one acquaintance, then the next—I don't remember whom. No, the sweater wasn't theirs. Then another inspiration: Joyce. I'd find out from her! Joyce was actually a college friend of my sister—that's how I'd gotten to know her. She was living up on the North Side and every week or so we'd go to Devon Street for a buffet lunch of tandoori chicken and vegetable curry. Joyce Richardson. At the very least the tone in her voice would tell me something—she was studying to be a therapist, but she hadn't yet learned the neutral tone.

I called her. Rehearsed and wooden, I began: "Joyce, I'd like to thank you for coming to the party ..."

She broke out in laughter. Several days earlier, we had talked about how nervous I was about the party, about how I expected that no one would actually come.

"You really are something," Joyce said, with lighthearted sympathy.

"You really are something"—the words seemed to echo.

But I knew I was nothing.

Suddenly, I saw myself through the eyes of others. In the eyes of the homeless man, I saw my own grandiosity and racism reflected back; in the eyes of the security guard and the woman at the cash register, I saw my composure unraveling; and in the eyes of the barman, I saw the image of someone who had lost himself so completely that he couldn't remember his own name.

Joyce didn't see me in that way, she couldn't—I wouldn't let her. She merely thought she was showing mercy to an insecure graduate student, not to a blackout drinker.

After I hung up the phone with Joyce, I realized that no one knew who I really was, not even me.

And so, I sat there, alone, with bottles all around me.

***

St. Augustine's *Confessions* is often passed around in recovery circles just as it is in Catholic ones: if you're a Catholic in recovery—it's required reading.

While everyone naturally focuses on Augustine's story in *Confessions*, I've always found Monica, Augustine's mother, to be the more interesting character. She's best known for relentlessly praying for Augustine's conversion—that's "praying Monica." But there's also another Monica, too, or at least another aspect of her: "drinking Monica," the patron saint of alcoholics. There's a scene in *Confessions* when Monica goes down to her wine cellar. Her maidservant looks at her, and says:

"Boozer."[1]

In *Confessions*, it's easy to see that Augustine is taken aback that a maidservant would speak to her mistress in that way; he observes that "boozer" was said not in a spirit of charity, but of condemnation.[2] But God, Augustine argues, was able to turn that ill will to good, and Monica never drank again. What Augustine was talking about is what Catholics call "actual grace," a supernatural impulse that allows us to act, to respond to God's call.

On that morning after the party, after sitting alone for a while, I went to the kitchen to get a phone book. I dialed the Alcoholism Helpline and said:

"I'm an alcoholic, and I need help."

It was a mercy to be able to say that—to admit what I had tried so long to hide. As my sobriety developed over the years, I would learn words to describe that experience: "moment of clarity," "jumping-off point," "powerlessness." Sometimes it's not that we're open to mercy as a conscious choice; it's that we *are opened* to mercy by circumstances beyond our own power to control or grasp. Grace is not automatic, of course, but sometimes it takes hopelessness for us to see that hope has existed all along, albeit in different ways than we were capable of imagining.

Stories of sobriety—like stories of conversion—are all different, but they're all the same. They're stories of mercy—stories about love and hope entering into the seemingly most desperate situations after we finally surrender to ourselves and to God.

I never did find out who owned the blue sweater or how it got on my couch. My memory and experience of looking at it so intensely stands in for those memories and experiences forever lost to the darkness of my drinking days.

But, like Monica, I never drank again—she had her wine cellar and I had my South Side apartment. I suppose we're all Monica in our own ways, with each of us having the metaphorical equivalent of a cellar where we hide and lock ourselves away.

But, like Augustine, I think I had a praying Monica, too: a person who understood my need in a sympathetic way, a praying Monica who noticed me, remembered me.

I believe we all have a praying Monica, even though she may be hidden from sight.

I'm sure that someone was praying for me: I had reached a place where only prayers could find me.

Suggested Questions for Discussion

1. What reaction do you have to the story? What feelings did you feel when reading it?
2. Is there a particular scene that stood out for you? Why did it stand out?

3. Mercy is mentioned at several junctures in the story—which is most interesting to you and why?
4. The end of the story mentions St. Monica, the mother of St. Augustine. How is she connected to the theme of mercy?

Suggested Questions for Private Reflection

1. If you saw yourself through the eyes of others, what would you see?
2. Is there a place you go—physically, mentally, or emotionally—where only prayers can find you? What would mercy mean there?

Chapter Two

Mercy and Reconciliation

Even now I don't know, exactly, why I bullied Zach.

"Hey, Mat, Mat Schmalz—get over here!"[1]

I recognized Zach out of the corner of my eye. I was surprised to see him at our twenty-fifth high school reunion in the summer of 2007.

I never even talked to Zach during our time at high school. Zach was part of my more distant past: the early 1970s, a time when I wore Toughskin jeans, flared at the cuffs and lazily hanging over my blue Keds sneakers. It was a time when I watched *Kukla, Fran, and Ollie* on Saturday mornings after *Fat Albert and the Cosby Kids*; it was a time when my favorite pastimes were playing army and exploring the woods behind my home. Zach and I had grown up in the same small town.

And Zach obviously remembered me.

I wondered how vivid and accurate his memories were.

I wondered whether Zach was planning to punch my face in.

***

I have a love/hate relationship with barbershops. Actually, the hate usually comes first. I just don't like how I look in the large barbershop mirror: doughy, with a dimple in the middle of my chin. I especially don't like it when the small mirror comes out so that the barber can show me the cut along the back of my neck.

All I see is me—reflected back infinite times.

I really don't like that.

But I do like the feeling of leaning back in the padded chair. And I do like the smells—dangerous as they are for me: the vaguely alcoholic scents of after-shaves and solvents mingling with the fruity aromas of newly cut, shampooed hair.

I went for a haircut before the reunion, anyway.

It was a barbershop by a gas station—the barber had brown coffee stains on his shirt, and I could see yellow tobacco residue on his fingernails as he picked up the shears. He moved vigorously and I closed my eyes to savor the feeling of falling hair lightly touching my eyelashes and clumping on my cheeks and chin.

"How does it look?" the barber asked in a raspy voice as he held up the mirror behind my head.

The haircut was shorter than I expected—shorter than I had asked for. I grimaced when I saw the moles and blotches on my scalp revealed for all to see. It had been third grade since my hair was that short.

Zach, he was the other guy in the class with hair as short as mine.

At the check-in at the hotel lobby, people started to recognize me. In making small talk, I had to maneuver around the memory of the last time I had actually seen most of them: it was at a party over winter break during my sophomore year in college. I use the word "seen" advisedly since I don't remember much of the night apart from crushing paper cups in my fist and popping balloons by stomping on them in my snow boots.

I started to feel uneasy, and I separated myself from the group.

Beyond the lobby there was a nondescript room where the cash bar had been set up. I passed through a set of sliding doors and couldn't help but notice how my crew-cut head reflected unevenly in the plate glass.

I wanted to put as much space as possible between me and the bar, so I went outside to the patio. There was a bar there, too—really a cart, with a beach umbrella more for appearances than for actual shade. I walked to where mortared gray stone gave way to a lawn and then long-grass fields, hills in the distance glowing blue and purple in the setting sun.

There was a railing separating the patio from the lawn—I hung onto it for support. I turned my back on the bar and kept my eyes on the hills.

That's where I heard Zach call my name.

***

The desks in our third-grade classroom weren't arranged in orderly rows. It was 1972, after all—and in Massachusetts, for good measure—and some of the experimental attitude of that time had filtered down to elementary school. Zach and I sat next to each other in a group of six desks that faced each other to make a kind of large table. The whole class was arranged like that—islands in a cinder block and linoleum sea.

Zach and I worked together in math. And I had something that helped us out—a special pen. I remember it clearly—its black cap and nib, and its fat green barrel. You'd just turn the cap and the multiples of numbers would peak through circular holes nicely arranged in a row. I shared the pen with Zach in class, and I think I even let him take it home once.

Zach and I also ran for president together. 1972 was an election year, and Zach and I were on the Republican ticket. He was Spiro Agnew to my Richard Nixon. I don't think we had to give speeches. We didn't know much about public policy or the Vietnam War, and Watergate was yet to come. But we had an election in class nonetheless, with a big map of the United States accompanying donkey and elephant stickers for states won by Democrats and Republicans.

Zach and I lost handily. Things were different for the real Nixon and Agnew—they won every state, every state except Massachusetts.

I acted up in school. My penmanship was terrible, so I'd throw my pencil. A letter came home from the gym teacher saying how I was failing: I had flat feet and "severe hand-eye coordination issues," which was a fancy way of saying that I couldn't catch a baseball. I remember one rainy day during a recess period inside: I busied myself by knocking down each and every chair in our classroom. I got sent to the office for that.

Zach would get on my nerves—and I told him so.

I didn't like his haircut—it was too much like mine. I didn't like his shirts, they were colorful and had fancy zippers—mine were usually a shade of blue or brown and I buttoned them right up to the top of my neck. I'd compare myself to Zach and say to him: "You look like a girl."

There was a tower in the middle of the school playground and we third-graders would race each other to the top. I wanted to make sure that Zach would never beat me, so I'd kick him, wrench his hand off the ladder, or try to push him off if he got ahead of me.

Then there were other things that I said and did to Zach. But I can't remember them.

But I do remember Zach's response, one time, when I was pressing my attack.

"I hate you, Mat."

I do remember that.

I'll always remember that.

***

"Hey, Mat Schmalz, get over here!" Zach repeated.

I finally turned round. There was Zach—standing there, nearly level with the fringe of the bar's beach umbrella.

His hair was close-cropped too—though there was a little more on the top of his head than mine.

No choice, I walked across the patio, looking down, measuring every step.

Zach's eyes were bright, big smile on his face. He switched his drink from right hand to left, stretched out his arm—for a second, I worried that he was going to grab the nape of my neck.

Instead, he gently clasped my shoulder.

He said, "I am so sorry."

I stood there, speechless.

"I am so sorry that I hit you in the fourth grade."

"I deserved it," I said—which was how I honestly felt even though I had absolutely no idea what Zach was talking about.

There were a couple of other onlookers standing around the bar, and so Zach explained. "Mat and I were doing a play in fourth grade."

Evidently, we got into some sort of argument and Zach hit me.

"It was a chicken scratch kind of thing," Zach said and held up his fingers, tensed and extended like a rooster's foot.

I'd like to say that Zach's description jogged my memory, but it didn't. I can imagine what happened, though. It must have been when I was engaging in some sort of verbal violence against Zach: teasing him, ridiculing him, shaming him—all the while probing for more weaknesses and vulnerabilities.

And I finally pushed Zach over the line. I'm sure I wanted to get a rise out of him in some way and just got more than I bargained for.

But Zach was the one who felt guilty. He clasped my shoulder a little more tightly and said to me: "I've been waiting thirty years to tell you I was sorry."

***

Sins are funny things—they have a long half-life. They hide, they wait, but they inevitably reemerge to get their own satisfaction— or our own comeuppance

Sin, of course, was a consistent feature of my Confraternity of Christian Doctrine classes—less formally known as Catholic Sunday school, though it was usually held on Monday evenings.

As the Baltimore Catechism puts it, "Actual sin is any willful thought, word, deed, or omission contrary to the will of God."[2] Although I couldn't have quoted catechetical literature verbatim in third grade, I did see that what I was doing was sinful.

I knew what I was doing—even though I was a child.

But I did not fully understand what I was doing either. Even now I don't know, exactly, why I bullied Zach. But what I can say is that Zach and I had that odd combination of similarities and differences that made connection and conflict possible. If I felt angry, unloved, frustrated, I found that I could make Zach share in those feelings.

At the reunion, Zach could have confronted me and told me how the wounds I inflicted on him healed, or did not heal, with time. He could have stuck to the dutiful small talk and perfunctory questions that so often characterize reunions and related functions like weddings and funerals. Zach could have ignored me altogether, very much like I might have ignored him if he had not pointed me out and called me by name.

But Zach chose to show me mercy.

The reunion continued with the whole class gathering round in a circle—it was time for awards: furthest distanced traveled, most times married, life of the party.

I stood shoulder to shoulder with Zach—we didn't win anything this time either.

***

What Zach did was merciful because he canceled a debt that I owed him. But he also did something more: he focused on our relationship—not just as we experienced it back in third and fourth grade, but also as we were experiencing it then and there. The mercy was a prelude to reconciliation, reestablishing a bond that was broken decades ago.

As the evening wound up and then wound down, I found myself circling back to Zach many times. We talked about work, about our families, and we mourned recently deceased classmates from our elementary-school days. Throughout our talks, Zach never mentioned once that I had bullied him.

Part of reconciliation is letting go—and I suppose Zach thought it was bad form to hold onto something negative about me from a time when we were kids. But there is something about the way we behave as children that prefigures the way we behave as adults. Our childhood cruelties often fester and metastasize into wounds or cancers that never fully heal. That's one reason I felt so guilty and ashamed about my treatment of Zach—it pointed to the person I could become with a drink in my hand.

So, I have to confess that I was glad that Zach didn't call me out for being a bully. I felt relief, and freedom. And I sat back and rested in that experience, letting it wash over me.

***

"Mat, it's Zach."

Zach had taken the initiative to call me. A couple of weeks earlier, I sent him an e-mail and apologized outright for bullying him in third grade.

It had been eight years since the reunion.

Mercy—like sin—is a funny thing. It also has a long half-life.

I'm not against apologies—I offer them quite liberally, actually. But I didn't apologize to Zach when I had the chance at the reunion. Being shown mercy is humbling; it exposes you and reflects back your vulnerabilities. I think I was feeling a little too exposed and vulnerable at the reunion to take the step that I should have taken in apologizing to Zach.

Apologies often cannot undo pain; but they can acknowledge it. Part of the cruelty of bullying is that the bruises it leaves are on the inside—it's a hidden form of violence, shrouded by shame. At the reunion, Zach showed he overcame his own shame and vulnerability—and his mercy to me finally proved stronger than the shame and vulnerability I carried inside myself. Reconciling with

Zach meant that I had to reconcile with my own self by taking responsibility for my actions, even though many years had passed. Mercy and reconciliation can lead to freedom and to new beginnings. But that freedom and those new beginnings do not include a free pass to forget.

Face to face with Zach once again—albeit virtually, on the telephone line—I repeated my apology: "Zach, I just wanted to tell you again how much it meant to me that you reached out at that reunion where we met a long while back. You apologized to me for giving me a hard time, when I should have been apologizing to you. I'm really sorry that I was such a bully."

"Well, you know my grandmother always taught me to turn the other cheek," Zach said, and then he chuckled. "If my grandmother had been allowed to be a priest, she'd have been the pope."

I laughed. Then I asked, "Do you remember running for president together back in third grade?"

"Oh, now you're really asking me to clear the cobwebs," Zach said, neither confirming nor denying my memory of things.

"We're much older now, Zach, aren't we?" I said. "Time is passing."

"It's the moments that matter—not the hours or the minutes," Zach reflected.

There was a pause and Zach added, "Back in third grade, I knew I could always talk to you."

Another pause. "And you'd listen—sometimes."

I laughed again.

"Just remember, I've always thought of you as a friend," Zach reminded me.

I smiled to myself as I hung up the phone. Zach's number was displayed on my handset—I made sure to write it down.

Suggested Questions for Discussion
1. What mindset and emotions can lead to bullying?

2. Do you agree with what Zach said in apologizing? Do you agree with him not calling the author out as a bully?
3. What do you think about how the author handled his meeting with Zach and why he acted the way he did?
4. How can mercy enable reconciliation between two people?

Suggested Questions for Private Reflection

1. If you were bullied as a child, or can imagine having been, what would it mean to bring mercy to that experience?
2. If you were a bully, or can imagine having been one, what could you do to reconcile with those whom you bullied?
3. If you were both bully and bullied—or again, can imagine such a situation—can you reflect on the relationship between the two?

Chapter Three

Mercy and Letting Go

"Let's get the story straight," I said.
"The night of the salmon burgers."

I'm not a handyman.

My older daughter, Veronica, can tell you that.

I tried fixing the toilet one time in our 1950s Massachusetts cape. As five-year-old Veronica supervised, I was able to remove the valve without much trouble, but I forgot to turn off the water. A waterspout shot up, almost hitting the bathroom ceiling. The cascade caught my left ear with a gurgle and whoosh, and drenched Veronica's pink sweat pants. She screamed and ran out of the bathroom into the waiting arms of her mother, my wife, Caroline, who had just navigated her way through the piles of clothes and books I had left on the stairs.

Veronica and Caroline then collapsed on the couch, shrieking with laughter.

"Oh, Daddy! Thank God it was clean toilet water!"

They laughed because I'm not a handyman.

To which my younger daughter, Joy, can also attest. I managed to slice and dice her yellow-flowered flip-flops when I ran them over with the lawn mower—luckily, she wasn't wearing them at the time. When she discovered the evidence of my misdeed, Joy gave me a pouty look and tears welled up in her eyes.

But she eventually forgave me because she realizes that I'm not a handyman.

Last and, of course, not least, Caroline can and certainly will tell you that I'm not a handyman. She's dreamed many dreams for me: from romantic imaginings of building a rock garden in our yard to more practical visions of fixing lamps and electrical outlets.

Caroline still dreams her dreams. But she's also understanding.

She accepts that I am not a handyman.

***

But I am a cook.

Veronica, Joy, and Caroline can tell you that. They hate to cook, but love to eat.

My specialty is Indian food. I'm comfortable with lentils, chickpeas, and lots of turmeric and garam masala. I can also do Italian—spinach lasagna is probably my best dish. I'm less handy with meat, but I can grill a steak and can manage a pork chop or tenderloin every now and then. Fish presents a special challenge—it's a little delicate whether fresh or frozen—and I'm not a finesse cook.

But I am a cook.

I fix breakfast, lunch, and dinner—and get the groceries for good measure. I know I don't repair things too well, and I make more messes than I clean up. But I've always thought that it's a mercy in our home that things are divided up in a way that we each do what we can.

***

As I remember it, things went like this:

It was winter. A *winter* Daddy-Day, the day I stayed home to take care of Veronica and Joy who then were about six and four years old, respectively—so it was about eight or nine years ago as I write now. Work that week had been draining. I was pre-tenure at my college, so I really felt under scrutiny: my every interaction with students and colleagues had a potentially cosmic significance that could affect my job prospects, and hence the life of my family. Daddy-Day was a brief respite from that—and a different experience of being a "provider." It also allowed Caroline to go to work at a local nature sanctuary.

On a normal day, everyone would wait for me to come home from work—I'd cook, and we'd have dinner. Things would be different if I was working after hours—attending a lecture, moderating a discussion, consulting with students about their papers in the library, on and on. On those days—which happened fairly frequently during those pre-tenure years—Caroline, Veronica, and Joy would have to fend for themselves.

In any case, it was Daddy-Day, and I was waiting for Caroline to come home so I could cook dinner. We'd then prepare our daughters for bed—read to them and watch them go to sleep. Afterward, I'd have some time to catch up on work.

I waited for Caroline. And I waited. It must have been at least an hour and a half. The kids were hungry. I was hungry. But more than that, my feelings were hurt. Dinner was something important, something that I could do beyond my job, part of my identity. I wanted to make it fresh; I didn't want to serve anything cold.

Caroline finally arrived. She entered with a big, "Hello, my beauties!" and the girls ran to hug her.

I was in the kitchen—still waiting—and moved to get some salmon burgers from the freezer.

I was silent—I might have said "Hi" to Caroline, nothing more, but I probably didn't even say that.

The salmon burgers were frozen together. It would be a meal that I could prepare quickly, but I needed to get the burgers apart. I jabbed a knife hard between two patties, then an expert flick of the wrist. But the knife slipped and caught my index finger. I glanced down: a bloody gash.

The cut looked deep.

"I have to go to the hospital," I said to Caroline. I was matter-of-fact, but I was serious. I grabbed a wad of paper towels and wrapped them around my finger.

The towels quickly became soaked bright red.

The urgency hit me.

"We have to go now!" I said.

Caroline got the kids together. Veronica and Joy picked up some storybooks as we exited the living room, went out the door, and navigated the slippery walkway to the car. We drove down to Urgent Care, near the University of Massachusetts Medical School and Hospital.

***

As Caroline remembers it, things went like this:

It was summer. A *summer* Daddy-Day—the one day when I would take care of the kids. The rest of days were hers with the kids, from morning until bedtime.

She was returning from work and arrived a half-hour late.

Given all the times that I arrived late, and given that this was her only day free from child-care responsibilities, it was a half-hour she felt entitled to. In any case, she knew, I'd drop most of the child-care duties once she got home, so Daddy-Day wasn't exactly a free day for Mommy.

She was hungry, looking forward to dinner. She hurried to the kitchen, excited to be home.

"You're late!" I shouted as I stabbed whatever I was cutting, stabbing myself in the process.

Then I said, "I need to go to the hospital for this cut."

As we were leaving the kitchen, she was so hungry from working for the day that she grabbed one leaf of a steamed artichoke and ate it.

She looked up to see me gazing at her with absolute disgust—as though she were putting her own petty need for sustenance before my own immediate need for medical attention.

So she put our toddler in the car seat and drove me to the Urgent Care Clinic.

***

When I first heard Caroline's version of "the night of the salmon burgers" I was surprised—and concerned. I thought that it was a relatively straightforward observation that Caroline and I had a rather merciful arrangement when it came to household chores— we both were in our comfort zones.

But our memories were so different, and it was clear that neither of us was feeling very merciful toward the other. This memory—thinking about it, talking about it—brought tensions to the surface that we avoided confronting.

Memories have blind spots—that much is certain.

Search the Internet or—if you have a little more time—explore any scientific database and you'll get reams of information about how people process information and record memories. Memories are flexible and fallible things: smells and sounds influence them as does diet—at least according to some studies. Maybe one reason why my memory and Caroline's differ is because we didn't have the opportunity to actually eat the salmon burgers—assuming I'm remembering the meal correctly—and get all those brain-building omega-3s.

But what's probably more to the point is that the content of a memory depends on the context when we recall it. We color our memories with distinctive emotional hues—it's not so much that we recollect memories as much as we paint them. Memories are landscapes and still lifes that portray our own sense of not necessarily how things were but how they must have been: certain elements stand out vividly while others are relegated to a shadowy background or an indeterminate space outside of the frame.

Marriages have blind spots, too.

In our busy lives, intimacy often becomes a set piece—we sit down and make time for discussions, for togetherness, for sharing. But sometimes the most intimate parts of ourselves—our desires, our fears, our needs and sensitivities—are revealed most strongly in the course of our mundane routines. Sharing in those daily activities can be the most profound experience, but it all too easily can become simply the experiencing of life side-by-side, mere coexistence. If you're distracted, if you're not in the moment, you often don't notice the obvious, let alone the often-coded communications that lie just below the surface of everyday life.

In thinking about how Caroline and I told the "night of the salmon burgers" story over the years, it was clear that we weren't just remembering things differently; we were also trying to give each other a message about the ways we needed mercy.

***

As I remember it, the hospital visit went like this.

I checked into Urgent Care close to 8:00 p.m., right before closing time. I showed my proof of insurance and paid the copay.

The waiting room was set up more for children—there were puzzles and storybooks with pictures of giraffes, elephants, and pandas.

I didn't have to wait long—the waiting room was almost empty.

First, a nurse practitioner saw me and took my blood pressure—it was very low. Sure sign of shock I thought.

Then came the doctor.

"I'm a professor at the College of the Holy Cross here in Worcester," I said, hoping to make a connection, to humanize myself—though maybe saying I was a husband and father would have been a better way of doing that.

"Really. I graduated from Holy Cross," the doctor said as he stretched a pair of latex gloves and put them on.

"I hope we treated you well." I really meant that—I didn't want a resentful doctor. I was splayed out on an examination table, my palm faceup to facilitate observation and probing. *I* certainly wanted to be treated well.

"Yes, great pre-med program." The doctor seemed genuine about that. I took a breath. The gloves were on and he was set. "I'm going to irrigate the wound," he stated.

Distilled water squirted into my cut.

"Ow!" Maybe I wasn't that dramatic, but it did sting.

He said, "Everyone has a different sensitivity to pain."

I wasn't sure whether this was a neutral observation or some sort of judgment. The doctor continued his work, making sure the wound was thoroughly cleaned.

I grunted. Tears came to my eyes.

"I can give you a shot."

"No—that's okay," I said, straining.

The blood had been washed off and the wound was now visible.

It was right along the line of the first joint on my left index finger—where the distal and middle phalanxes meet.

The wound wasn't very wide. It wasn't very long. It didn't go very deep.

I could see the doctor was weighing the options, quickly measuring them in his mind.

He said: "It's a tough decision—whether or not to give you a stitch. Maybe some surgical tape would work fine."

I wanted a stitch. I deserved one. But I was also starting to feel a little embarrassed.

I went ahead and asked for a stitch—sheepishly, apologetically, softly.

And I got it—a single stitch, a small suture, expertly tied off by the doctor who wished me the best as I went on my way.

Caroline and our girls were in the waiting room. Joy and Veronica were running around between the puzzle table and the pile of storybooks. Caroline was in a chair, droopy-eyed and clearly out of breath.

***

We don't have full family meetings very often, at least not formal ones, except when Caroline is organizing a house cleaning and we have to get focused on our jobs. But I had decided to write about the "night of the salmon burgers" because I wanted to find its merciful core. I felt a meeting was in order to set the record straight about what actually happened, beyond Caroline and me relying on our own individual stories in isolation.

I yelled up to Veronica who was in her room working on a short story or texting or sleeping. "Veronica, come down here, please." Joy was already in the living room—she's permanently claimed the recliner where she reads or watches arts-and-craft videos on YouTube. Caroline was on the couch, handling email correspondence.

"We have to talk," I said after Veronica came downstairs and we were all gathered together.

My laptop was ready. Caroline and Veronica were perched on the couch expectantly—Joy hadn't moved from the recliner. I noticed that our family setup was triangular. "We have to triangulate our memories," I said. "Like explorers trying to determine our position in the wilderness by extrapolating from established landmarks!" Everyone stared at me blankly.

"Let's get the story straight," I said. "The night of the salmon burgers."

Caroline sighed. "I was a vegetarian then—it couldn't have been salmon burgers."

"I think it was turbot," Veronica said.

"Turbot," I said. "A cold-water flatfish harvested off the coast of Greenland. Trader Joe's carried it regularly in the frozen seafood section, so that's possible, Veronica. But turbot doesn't require very much knife work. Like, none."

"Plus, Veronica, you weren't even there—you're just pretending you were," Joy said. Then: "I *was* there and don't remember anything about it."

"I walked you around while Daddy was with the doctor," Caroline added. "You were interested in *everything*, and I had to keep you safe. I didn't even have a chance to sit down."

Harold, our big black poodle with an inordinate need for affection, was making his rounds, sitting in front of each one of us in turn and prodding us with his snout, hoping—no, expecting—to be gently scratched and petted.

We started laughing—all of us.

We laughed hard.

"Daddy got a mercy stitch," Caroline said.

We agreed on that.

And laughed even harder.

***

Facts stand behind memories: things happened or they didn't. We can say the same thing about behavior: our actions were sensitive or insensitive; our attitudes were kind or selfish. In marriages, certain arrangements are fair or unfair; certain assumptions are balanced or biased. And we tell ourselves we know which are which.

But as a family we really had differing ideas about which was which.

Talking through family dynamics is important—it's a way of doing the hard work of making sure that our perceptions are in line with our behavior. But all too easily, those kinds of discussions can devolve into argument and acrimony. It was becoming apparent at our family meeting that Caroline and I were still resentful toward each other—and conditions were ripe for escalation, both of us trying to vindicate our memories and feelings. I felt under-appreciated; Caroline felt overburdened. I felt as though I was being dismissed; Caroline felt as though she were being set up.

Underlying all of that were the different ways men and women—husbands and wives—see and value not only themselves but also each other.

Caroline and I could have really had it out right then and there. And Veronica and Joy would have probably fled the scene and taken Harold with them.

But we laughed instead.

Laughter can be cruel and dismissive, but it can also be a way of letting go: letting go of the need to stand by oneself; letting go of the barriers we place in front of those who try to connect with us; letting go of the need to argue, to be right, to communicate a definitive message that everyone has to hear and accept.

And letting go is indeed a mercy because it is a way of *letting in* other possibilities—especially when we find ourselves stuck in situations where what we're doing promises only further conflict and pain.

I suppose saying that I got a "mercy stitch" was a way of acknowledging that I took myself pretty seriously as a cook. But it was also a way of acknowledging that my way of looking at things was skewed—out of proportion, out of touch.

I'm definitely not a handyman.

That we could all laugh about it was the mercy stitch we needed as a family—a mercy stitch that brought us closer by tying together our memories and tying off our real and imagined wounds.

Suggested Questions for Discussion

1. What are the ways you feel most comfortable contributing to your family? Where do you struggle?
2. What kinds of things in your family life do you have to be reminded about? What might be your blind spots?
3. Have you ever experienced a "mercy stitch" situation when you overreacted to something?
4. In what kind of situations can laughter be merciful?

Suggested Questions for Private Reflection

1. What are specific ways you can bring mercy into tensions or hurt feelings in your family life?

2. Do you sometimes communicate your feelings in coded ways? If so, what could you do to be clearer and more upfront?

Chapter Four

Mercy and Compassion

We Catholics carry a lot of baggage—purses and wallets
crammed with emotional IOUs and invoices
for promises made but never kept.

"Go easy on yourself."

"Give yourself a break."

"Don't get down on yourself."

"Don't beat yourself up."

We've all heard these expressions a lot, sentiments that fit in nicely with our cultural assumptions. Mercy to yourself can be a form of "me time," a way of focusing on personal needs we may have ignored or neglected. Mercy to yourself can be a way of tuning out and plugging in: recharging your batteries by connecting to private sources of energy—things like listening to the surf while walking on the beach, feeling the wind in your hair during a bike ride, or savoring the guilty pleasure of eating an extra piece of cake or a fat bag of potato chips.

"Go easy on yourself."

It's a terrible idea—a dangerous idea—at least that's what I'd always thought. People should hold themselves to a standard.

***

I have this list—a mental list.

There's the bully who gave me a wedgie in seventh grade—pulled my underwear up and out so the whole gym class could see. He's an executive for a Fortune 500 company now. His name is on the list.

46

There's the scholar who moaned and groaned about how poorly I was editing a volume, but then never submitted a publishable chapter. He happens to publish more in a year than I'll publish in a lifetime. Just not with me. His name is on the list.

There are disruptive students and difficult colleagues, ex- and would-have-been girlfriends, noisy neighbors, jerky journalists, and that counter person at Dunkin' Donuts who didn't listen to me and put sauce on Joy's flatbread-sandwich disaster. Their names are all on the list.

It's a list of people who never apologized to me; it's list of people who were too merciful with themselves.

A lot of people have lists like I do. But I don't find that a comforting thought.

I feel guilty about having a list at all.

Caroline's grandfather had an actual physical list of people who had wronged him: he wanted to be sure that he wouldn't forget everyone he was mad at. He died on a barstool, with the list in his pocket.

I certainly don't want to be like that.

Jesus obviously wasn't too enthused about the whole list thing. He said, "Judge not, that you be not judged" (Mt 7:1). Clear and uncompromising words, to be sure. But maybe there's also something else going on—a suggestion, perhaps, that not being able to show mercy to others is connected to not being able to feel mercy toward yourself.

"Go easy on yourself."

"Give yourself a break."

"Don't get down on yourself."

"Don't beat yourself up."

Thinking through what all of that might mean doesn't provide much quick satisfaction—the "mercy to yourself" route is a lot simpler when you just kick back and grab that extra piece of cake or the fat bag of potato chips.

***

Caroline ran her fingers through her thick, silver hair, looked at me with her hazel eyes, and gave me a freckly smile after she put down the phone. "I'm going to work at the nature sanctuary tomorrow. You can go into your man cave."

The next morning we had coffee in the living room—I was on the small couch, its upholstery frayed by my habit of grinding and burrowing my feet into the cushions; Caroline sat perpendicular to me on an IKEA sofa. The only sounds were the clicks of our computer keyboards and the occasional wheezing of Harold the poodle. Veronica and Joy were away with Caroline's parents in New Jersey, indulging in the extravagances that only grandparents can give.

It was a summer day and here was my chance to enact the experiment I'd been considering, a chance to control the variables—to make sure the experiment would be just about me.

I was going to figure out what it meant to be merciful to myself.

After a while, Caroline closed up her computer and said, "Honey, I got to go." She straightened her nametag on her navy blue shirt and smoothed her chinos. Harold raised his head slightly. I nodded and waved to Caroline from my prone position, cradling the laptop on my chest.

I had already made my man cave.

It was going to be my mercy day.

***

I woke up a couple hours later with no clearer idea about what a guy should do on his mercy day. I made myself some toast and coffee, then more coffee. I looked at the television and it occurred to me that I could binge watch something. But then I thought about a sign that Caroline's late grandmother had on her television:

"Would Jesus watch this show with you?"

I had to admit that most of the shows I would be inclined to watch were not Jesus-friendly.

I closed my eyes again.

And the list appeared.

More often than not, it's the Catholic stuff that makes it to the top. In my opinion, Catholics should hold themselves to a higher standard.

Father Thompson led the list on my mercy day.

Father Thompson—he was one tough priest. He would deny children baptism if their parents weren't regular churchgoers. He was old school: you'd address him by his last name; his favorite pope was Pius XII, the last pope before the Second Vatican Council.

And Father Thompson was my confirmation sponsor. He was the one who put his hand on my shoulder when the bishop anointed me with chrism oil and I took the name Thomas—the doubter, the Apostle to India—as my confirmation name. But over thirty years, Father Thompson had never contacted me.

That hurt.

Of course, there's a little more to the story, as I gradually remembered, lying there on the couch. I had written to Father Thompson, usually at five-year intervals. And he did write back—most of the time. But he was on my list because he never initiated getting in touch, never checked in to see how I was doing.

Was the priest who refused to give the mercy of baptism giving himself mercy a little too easily?

Or maybe I was the one who wasn't being merciful enough. After all, Father Thompson was pretty old now—almost one hundred years old, actually. It seemed cruel to still be angry with him.

I lay there on the couch, stewing in resentment and guilt.

Slowly, inevitably, I was forced to confront something that I had been avoiding with all my lying down. And it was probably the real reason that Father Thompson made it to the top of the list on my mercy day.

I needed to go to confession.

***

Along with baptism, confession is Catholicism's preeminent rite of mercy. I can graph important transitions in my life by experiences I have had in the confessional. In high school and college, I used to go to confession with Father Joseph Quigley, head of the Newman Center at the University of Massachusetts and the chaplain at Amherst College, where I went to school. Whenever confession would conclude, he'd say, "We're proud of you." It was a phrase he always used with us students—it's a phrase that I use with the students I teach now.

So, confession is not a fear-filled experience for me. I did have one rocky time though—I went to confession with a bishop and proceeded to debate what sins should be classified as venial and which should be classified as mortal. Confession is the place to confess, not to argue, I found out. In any case, the idea of confession is something that I readily accept as being important and healthy.

At the same time, over the years, my participation in confession had become rather sporadic. Officially, Catholics are required to go to confession at least once a year (see *Catechism of the Catholic Church*, 2042). But there were many years, after graduate school and during the early years of my marriage and work, when I didn't go at all.

Part of the reason for that lies in the dynamics of being a Catholic, which means not just being involved with the institution but dealing with people.

And people can disappoint you.

Sometimes I think every Mass is a setup for some kind of disappointment. You get up on a Sunday morning and rouse the kids, making it to church just in the nick of time. Then you have to contend with the woman sitting on the edge of the pew who just won't make room for you. If you have a non-Catholic spouse or relative with you, there's usually no effort made to welcome them and no information to explain what's actually going on. Then if you want to actually pray or meditate after Mass, you have to close your eyes and ears to the rush to the parking lot that begins as soon as Communion ends.

Those small things add up.

Then there are the bigger things, the weightier matters.

The sexual-abuse scandal cut into the very heart of parish life and the relationship laity have with their priests, their leadership, and one another. I myself have known six priests who were implicated in sexual-abuse scandals. I found out about them not through any personal communication from a parish or religious order, but by reading media reports or looking online at document dumps that dioceses had made when required by law.

I myself hadn't been abused, but when I heard the revelations I felt keenly the betrayal of my trust.

We Catholics carry a lot of baggage: suitcases and backpacks stuffed with souvenirs of hurt; satchels and briefcases filled with spreadsheets tallying offenses; purses and wallets crammed with emotional IOUs and invoices for promises made but never kept. And when Catholics consider going to confession—or to church—they often have to figure out what to do with that baggage. Not being able to carry that baggage—or to leave it behind—is one reason why people stay home.

***

I chose to go to a place where the priest did not know me. That would work well with the experimental ethos of my mercy day. I was going to see how someone responded to me as a blank slate.

I started up my old green Toyota—it's pockmarked from a hailstorm a while back. If the drive to the church had been longer, I might have found an excuse to turn around: a warning light on the dashboard, perhaps, or heavy traffic, or maybe even another hailstorm. The drive only took five minutes.

St. Agatho's was small and open, a comforting feeling. I remembered fondly my devout teenage years when I could stop and pray in any church I was walking by. St. Agatho was a man, not a woman—I knew that much, but no more about him or the church that bears his name. I opened St. Agatho's glass doors and saw that the church wasn't exactly empty—a couple of members of the choir were practicing on a balcony just over the entrance to the main aisle.

I knelt down in one of the middle pews—they were painted white and the interior of the church had a Massachusetts colonial feel. There were green banners, and white and pink flowers framed the golden tabernacle. I prayed an Our Father and a couple of Hail Marys. I looked around—it was unclear where the confessional was.

That's a good excuse to leave, I thought. No provision made for newcomers. But before my resentment could reach full boil, the parish priest came to the altar and motioned to a door off to the side.

I was being invited to go to confession.

I went in the room and sat on a wooden chair in front of the priest. He wore street clothes and a green woolen stole. The priest did not stare right into my eyes, he simply bowed his head slightly and turned his right ear toward me.

I confessed my sins

There were no sparks, no fire and brimstone, and no voices from on high.

But it was confession.

For Catholics, confession is a sacrament: it symbolizes and makes real the forgiveness of sins. It's not like therapy, but the "talk" aspect of confession is still important: the exchanges that happen in the context of confession—whether face-to-face or through a sliding screen—are a crucial part of the mercy that leads us to reestablish a personal relationship with God.

The priest and I talked about my list, because what I had to confess concerned how my resentments were a stumbling block for me, how I just couldn't get past the anger and the guilt.

"Whenever you feel a resentment, it's a call to compassion," the priest suggested gently. He referred to the story of Elijah, which was part of that Sunday's Scripture readings, and how Elijah fasted and journeyed to Mount Horeb over forty days (see 1 Kgs 19:1-8). The number forty is associated with rebirth, with new life—and with long, seemingly impossible, quests.

"It's going to take time to work through these things," the priest said, softly.

I nodded. I wasn't exactly the prophet Elijah fleeing the Baal-worshiping Queen Jezebel, but the idea of rebirth struck a chord with me.

"Here's what you can do for your penance," he continued. "I want you to say five Our Fathers, and when you say them, try to channel compassion to those you feel have hurt you."

I said a brief Act of Contrition. In confession, contrition is the prayer that you say to God, in the presence of the priest, to express sadness for your sins and your intent not to sin again. I had re-memorized a longer form before I set off for church, but I actually lost my train of thought at the end of the confession: I was thinking about how anger, guilt, and compassion related to mercy—my mind was whirling. So I said a spontaneous expression of sorrow and resolution to amend.

I then went to kneel in the pew to perform my penance.

In church, I usually pray with my eyes open because it's a way of going outside of myself. Depending on where I'm kneeling, I connect with the crucifix or a statue of Mother Mary, or focus on the symbolism on the door of the tabernacle. This time I had my eyes closed—because this time it was an internal landscape I was trying to create and connect with.

I said an Our Father, slowly and in rhythm with my breathing. After that first Our Father, I visualized the red-haired bully I knew in seventh grade. He was on my mind because I had just written a draft about Zach and me and it brought up memories of when I was bullied too.

I said—internally—"I give you my compassion." I wasn't sure what I even meant, exactly. I knew that redhead was a big pot-smoker back in seventh grade—maybe I should be compassionate about that, maybe in some way he needed mercy in his life at that time. Maybe.

I said another Our Father, slowly and in rhythm with my breathing. I named and visualized that scholar who gave me difficulties with the volume I was editing. I was actually the one who cut him loose when it was clear that we weren't working well together and that he really didn't want to contribute any longer. We both began with the best of intentions, however. He was an established professor who only got involved with the project because he was trying to do me a good turn.

I said—internally—"I give you my compassion."

At that point, something didn't feel right. "I give you my compassion" might work if I was sitting on a throne and holding court—but I was on my knees in front of the altar. It just seemed like a really highhanded way to express myself.

How was mercy to myself related to compassion for others?

"Compassion" is something more than sympathy—I knew that much. Literally, compassion means "co-suffering," "suffering with someone."

I paused and tried to think things through.

When the priest made the connection between resentments and compassion, I think he was calling attention to a dynamic of mutual suffering that so often shapes how and why people hurt each other and then cannot let it go. Compassion is a form of mercy: it's being present with another in suffering.

I thought about Father Thompson.

He was a tough guy, but he also had a tough time—especially with those of us in the younger generation. He didn't know popular music—he called it "the bouncy stuff teenagers like." He didn't follow sports teams. He didn't even own a television.

Father Thompson did know about Latin America—he had spent years in Colombia. But he was often told to stay in the United States—to stay running parishes that certainly had their needs, but nowhere near the range of needs that parishes in rural Colombia had. Although Father Thompson had his own disappointments with authority in the Church, and with conventional parish life in America, he was obedient to his superiors and tried his best with us kids. He answered every single question I ever asked about the ins and outs of Catholic doctrine—from hell to heaven, from angels to assisted suicide.

And he answered "yes" when I asked him if he would be my confirmation sponsor.

I was now hurt, because I admired him—I was resentful because I loved him.

So it was with most of the names on my list—even the red-headed bully. They were people I wanted to be close to—people I liked and wanted to like me. We had complex, often confusing, relationships that were shaped not just by admiration but also by envy and by often unspoken needs and expectations.

Compassion is co-suffering—recognizing and experiencing the interconnectedness of love and longing, anger and disappointment. Mercy comes in when you accept the whole thing—and the whole person.

***

I concentrated on compassion as "co-suffering." Instead of emphasizing the suffering, I decided to put the emphasis on the "co"—on the "with."

I said a third Our Father, slowly and in rhythm with my breathing. I named and visualized Father Thompson. I said—internally—"I make space for you."

I wasn't sure exactly where that particular line came from, though it did have a familiar ring. In any case, it rang true. Compassion is a way of making space for others and sharing in the complexity of their lives.

Compassion is also a way of making space for ourselves: co-suffering with the parts of ourselves that are hurt or injured, which we would otherwise deny or ignore. Being compassionate in this way is a form of mercy of the most authentic kind, embracing our full humanity, with all its vulnerabilities and limitations.

There, sitting in the pew and performing my penance, I was able to focus my mind's eye and see the elderly Father Thompson.

Standing with him, I also saw my younger self: curious, but needy—and always prone to going to extremes. One time, I even yelled at Father Thompson when he didn't thank me for bringing the mail in while he was away. I remember I stormed out of the rectory and slammed the door so hard that I feared the glass panels would crack and shatter.

Father Thompson and I were both awkward and wounded in our own ways, but we were both connected, joined. Whatever resentment I felt wasn't just about him—or about me—but it was about both of us. And I sensed the heavy weight of my feelings somehow lightening and lifting.

I repeated the prayer two more times, naming and visualizing a colleague who I thought had let me down and a longtime friend who tried to get me to drink again. After the prayers, I didn't feel free, exactly—but I did feel free enough.

I sat silently for a time. Then I crossed myself, genuflected before the tabernacle, and left for home.

On the drive back, I felt good about giving confession another chance. It was certainly an experience of "compassion"—of "co-suffering"—in the best sense: a way of fully being present to God, to another human being, and to my often confused and conflicted feelings about myself and others.

But I still wasn't sure exactly what to do with my list. One thing was clear to me, however. In keeping a mental list, I wasn't writing down names, I was writing people off.

***

My mercy day ended much as it had begun—with me on the couch.

As an introverted professor type, I'm good with abstractions and mulling things over in my mind in any number of ways. The whole idea of compassion and mercy as making space seemed really clever to me. In a lot of my scholarly writing, I talk about space: social space, imaginative space, existential space, and so on. A list is something regimented, and what I was moving toward was a different kind of template for understanding the intersections of anger and guilt, and all the variables that surround them. I thought that the notion of compassionately sharing space with someone might work well as a kind of three-dimensional graph of mercy.

Seeing things in that way might be an interesting academic exercise.

But lying there on the couch, it occurred to me that my thoughts were probably "academic" in the sense of being removed or maybe even useless. Mercy and compassion, sharing space with someone—these were connections that I made after I had been alone most of the day. My day was supposed to be about experience, not theory.

I thought about Caroline. She was respecting my inclination to retire to my man cave for some alone time. She was making space for me, by allowing me my own space.

But I still could have made space for her, surprising her at work, for example, or at least giving her a call.

I could have made Caroline part of my mercy day.

I felt guilty again.

"Go easy on yourself."

"Give yourself a break."

"Don't get down on yourself."

"Don't beat yourself up."

It's easier to say those things to yourself—and believe them—when you realize that mercy isn't a solitary pursuit but a compassionate act to let other people in.

There's always another chance—as long as you don't write people off.

Harold started barking and jumped up on the couch to look out the window.

Caroline had returned.

I got off the couch and went outside to help with her belongings, making sure that the door was open so we could both walk through together. Afterward, maybe we could talk some, and treat ourselves to an extra piece of compassion or a fat bag of mercy.

Suggested Questions for Discussion

1. How do you handle hurt and disappointment?
2. What do you think "be merciful to yourself" means? What kinds of acts or experiences come to mind?
3. How does your experience in the Catholic Church shape your understanding and experience of compassion?
4. What are specific ways you can be merciful to yourself that include other people?

Suggested Questions for Private Reflection

1. Who's on *your* list? What kind baggage do you carry around?
2. What would be a merciful and compassionate way to deal with the names on your list and the baggage you carry?

PART TWO

MERCY AND OTHERS

Chapter Five

Mercy and Freedom

"It's your responsibility to set up an operation so I can get my eyesight back," Ghura Paul told me.

I first met Ghura Paul in 1985.[1]

Ghura Paul was standing by a hand pump, bathing and washing his clothes. His arms were muscled and his shoulders broad. He yelled out to me a hearty, "Jai Yesu," the Hindi greeting used by Catholics in North India, meaning "Hail Jesus."

Ghura Paul lived in a village near a Catholic mission that I was visiting during my college junior year abroad in India. The Catholic mission was a landmark in the area—it had a brick rectory for priests, a school, and a convent for nuns who administered a medical dispensary and clinic.

The mission was established by Canadian Capuchins in the late 1940s and then shifted in 1962 to the Indian Missionary Society, an Indian Catholic religious order. The 1960s were a time of famine in North India when Catholics surrounding the mission supplemented their food rations with an improvised energy drink made of sugar-cane husks, tobacco leaves, and water. By 1985, conditions had improved—the mission had built wells and roads throughout the area so that there was a sufficient infrastructure for cultivation. Most Catholic converts worked the local wheat fields, earning one bundle of wheat for every sixteen they gathered. Some Catholic families were also "bonded laborers" and worked as virtual slaves to repay high-interest debts held over them by wealthy landowners.

Catholics belonged to what was then known as the Untouchable Chamar caste of tanners. They were socially ostracized because they were considered so polluted that they could not even be touched by others. While Untouchability still persists in Indian society, the term "Untouchability," along with "Untouchable," is now considered to be controversial and offensive—the preferred and politically conscious word used by members of Untouchable castes to describe themselves is "Dalit," meaning "oppressed" or "crushed."

Ghura was a name befitting that oppressive and crushing social status—it meant "dung heap," though the translation that best expresses its impact would be "pile of shit." Paul was his baptismal name, which he chose when he converted to Catholicism as a young man.

**

I next met Ghura Paul in 1995.

I was living at the mission and wearing what I usually wore: a long collarless shirt, billowy white pants, and sandals. I rode my rickety bicycle along the main road, carefully moving to the side to avoid speeding trucks and then picking up my pace to overtake bullock carts and the occasional water buffalo. The road took me by wheat fields and mango orchards. There didn't seem to be much development over the past ten years—still no tractors, for example, and most homes were built of mud and thatch. I turned down a dusty cobblestone path that cut through a small bazaar with tea stalls and vegetable sellers. I coasted and veered right, toward the Ganges River.

Unlike other Catholics, Ghura Paul had a multi-room home, made of brick—it was easy to find. Ghura Paul was sitting outside on a rope bed. He was barefoot and bare-chested, wearing a long white homespun cloth tied around his waist and elegantly pleated and folded in the front so it gave the appearance of pant legs. The priest at the mission, Father Sanchit, told me about the acid attack that blinded Ghura Paul several years earlier. But I was still shocked—scars cascaded from Ghura Paul's head to his torso, and half his right ear was burned off.

"Jai Yesu," I said.

"Jai Yesu," Ghura Paul replied as he prayerfully folded his hands in front of his chest to greet me. He motioned for me to sit next to him on the rope bed.

I mentioned our meeting a decade earlier, but he didn't remember it. "I'm writing my Ph.D. dissertation on the local Catholic community," I said.

"I hear you're from America," Ghura Paul said—clearly having been briefed about my arrival. "The mission used to receive a lot of goods from America."

I probably said "haan," the Hindi word for "yes," instead of shaking my head side to side as would have been the normal custom.

"I can still sense light, you know," Ghura Paul said as he pointed to his eyes. I realized that his eyes hadn't opened since we had been talking: they were permanently closed because the skin of his eyelids had bonded to the skin surrounding his eye sockets—a condition clinically described as "total symblepharon."

"It's your responsibility to set up an operation so I can get my eyesight back," Ghura Paul told me.

I felt trapped, offended, and potentially responsible. I stammered in Hindi, "I'll try."

"No, you will not try. You'll do it," Ghura Paul insisted.

I heard the rhythm of saris being pounded against flat washing stones. I looked beyond Ghura Paul and over the waist-high stone wall bounding the courtyard, toward the sandy banks of the Ganges River.

***

Over the next sixteen months, I spent many hours with Ghura Paul, recording and translating his songs and poems that wove together Christian and Hindu imagery. We also were companions of a sort. Every month we took a bus to a Catholic prayer center in the city of Varanasi about eighty miles south.

I remember our first visit well. Ghura Paul took a white cloth and wrapped it around his head and face so that no one would ask about his scars. We waited fitfully for the bus on the main road. Usually, when boarding a bus in India no quarter is given, you have to elbow your way on and wedge yourself in. But the conductor recognized that Ghura Paul might need assistance, so he yelled for us to wait.

"I'm blind, not deaf!" Ghura Paul said defiantly.

The conductor and his assistant came down and placed their hands on Ghura Paul's back and buttocks.

Ghura Paul protested as he was shoved into the bus: "I'm blind, not lame!"

He stood in the aisle for the next six hours.

We arrived at the charismatic prayer center as everyone was leaving—we had missed everything. After a brief rest and a cup of tea, I took Ghura Paul's hand and led him back to the bus stand so we could get back to his village by nightfall.

I didn't do a very good job as guide. Ghura Paul stubbed his foot on a rock and fell, though we did manage to get to the bus.

Over the next few weeks, I rode my bike to explore the villages surrounding the mission. I got to know the Catholic community. It was pretty spread out, but most Catholics lived in what were euphemistically called "labor colonies" on the outside of villages where they had set up bamboo and palm-leaf lean-tos near the wheat and rice fields.

Each morning, I would begin at Ghura Paul's home. We practiced walking together on the cobblestone path in front of his house. He would lightly hold my hand and move according to whether I kept my arm straight or shifted it to the left or to the right.

Our next journey to the prayer center was uneventful, and we actually arrived on time. During the prayer service, I led Ghura Paul to the stage. He stood in front of a large cardboard cutout of a Caucasian Christ. The audience was large, nearly a thousand people, predominately women dressed in brightly colored saris—electric pink, lime green, and orange. Ghura Paul could hear them, especially as the crescendo of prayers grew when he stepped forward toward the microphone.

Bluntly, Ghura Paul told everyone to be quiet. He was wearing dark glasses, but everyone knew he was blind. He stood behind the microphone at the podium and began, his Hindi loud and confident: "I was a Communist who believed in revolution, but I heard Jesus' message of love." He then recounted how he fought nonviolently for the poor as headman of his village.[2]

"That's why the landowners—and some of my own people—threw acid on me while I was sleeping."

A cry went up from the audience.

By his "own people" Ghura Paul meant his fellow Catholics.

I had been actively researching the rumors about who perpetrated the attack against Ghura Paul.[3] Some Catholics near the mission had told me that it was Ghura Paul's neighbors and family members who were incensed at his abuses of power—including his sexual advances toward their wives, sisters, and daughters. Other people said that it was henchmen of the area's landowners who feared the growing political power of a Dalit who was also Christian.

I didn't have a provable theory of who was behind the attack then. I don't now. All that was clear to me is that perceptions of who was behind the attack reflected the caste divisions and prejudices in the area—everyone had a vested interest in blaming someone.

But Ghura Paul did not delve into that backstory as he gave his testimony from the stage. Instead, he raised his hands and proclaimed: "I have forgiven my attackers. God is an ocean of mercy!"

Women in the audience also raised their hands and began to pray in tongues for mercy for Ghura Paul's attackers and for Ghura Paul himself. I also thought that many were surely praying for mercy for the many victims of violence they knew from their own villages and families.

***

For decades, the Indian government has pursued an extensive affirmative-action program to reintegrate Dalits into society: positions in government jobs and universities are reserved for Dalits and elected positions are as well. But Ghura Paul was also a Catholic Christian, and Christian members of Dalit castes are legally barred from receiving governmental benefits. For this reason, Catholic missions had long provided food and other forms of aid.

Eventually, the Catholic Church came to be seen as a store or factory that simply handed out material goods. Wanting to battle that impression, the Catholic mission in Ghura Paul's area drastically reduced the aid it distributed.

A letter from the priest of the charismatic prayer center arrived at the mission. It was addressed to Father Sanchit, but inquired whether I—as a presumably affluent American—could be of any help in providing an operation for Ghura Paul. The letter didn't mention mercy explicitly, but that's what it was really about. It was about giving Ghura Paul a second chance—and who should give it to him.

Father Sanchit called me in to the refectory. Sugary milk tea had been prepared by the cook and was waiting for us on a big black table. Sweet biscuits and salty snacks—crispy fried lentils and pretzels made of chickpea flower—completed the setting. Father Sanchit read me the letter and then set it aside. "We can't do this," he said. "Can you imagine the rush of people who would come for help? There'll be a chain reaction if the mission gives

Ghura Paul anything—it would be impossible to provide for every need in an area where so many people are suffering. We'd be overwhelmed."

I shook my head side to side, indicating agreement.

"Whatever resources we have, we should use to help the greatest number—not a single person who's already had his chance."

I probably shook my head in agreement again and kept sipping tea, but I was worried about how this all would impact me.

Father Sanchit bit into a biscuit and said: "Once, not so long ago, when Ghura Paul was headman, Father Khrist Bhakt went to him to ask for his assistance when a local Catholic colony had burned to the ground. Ghura Paul made the priest wait three hours before telling him that he couldn't—he wouldn't—do anything."

"Ghura Paul has learned nothing from experience," Father Sanchit concluded, putting his teacup down with a clatter. "Even if he gets his eyesight back—he'll still be blind."

That was harsh, I thought. I finished my tea and grabbed a fistful of fried lentils, feeling the salt and spices sear my mouth as I chewed.

***

Evaluating someone's openness to mercy? That made me uncomfortable—and still does. After all, one understanding of mercy is that it's precisely something that is unmerited, if not unasked for. But we all have found—or will find—ourselves in situations where something is either asked of us or needed from us. In those situations, there are certain inevitable questions that we ask: What are my responsibilities? What is the real need? Am I able to do something that helps rather than harms? And, perhaps most importantly, what are my own motivations?

That last question was particularly troubling for me as my relationship with Ghura Paul developed.

One time, when we were sharing a room at the prayer center, I pressed him for another song that I could record and translate.

"You'll have to wait," Ghura Paul said. "I want to stay here a couple more days—after that, maybe."

So we stayed. The prayer center was comfortable enough. Ghura Paul and I had a clean room with two rope beds; a bathroom with a squat toilet was a short walk away; and we could bathe and do our laundry under a tap outside. Ghura Paul sat for many hours on a stone bench in the prayer center's garden, sometimes joined by me and at others times by a noisy flock of peacocks and peahens that made their home amid the coconut palms and banyan trees.

"I've composed a drama," Ghura Paul said to me after our breakfast of curried chickpeas, yogurt, and flatbread. We had managed to stay three days beyond what we had initially planned, but the prayer center was open to all who arrived, and everyone was free to stay as long as they wanted.

Ghura Paul explained the drama: "It will be long. If it was going to be actually performed, it would take hours, with all the traveling, eating, and such." It was a story about a pilgrimage to a shrine dedicated to Our Lady. Ghura Paul narrated it to me, and it concluded with one character's plaintive plea to the Blessed Virgin. Ghura Paul's voice was deep but cracked when he sang the words "Mother Mary," *Mata Mariam*, in Hindi:

Please keep me with you,
And I will sing your name all of my life
Oh, Mother Mary
I do not need food or money, gold or silver
I will give up all my money without delay
And also give you the skin off my body
So that on one day
A slave of yours will be born
Without a son I have become disgraced
I am now called a barren woman

Oh, please stay with me, Mother Mary
And I will sing your praises my whole life[4]

It was scholarly gold. And I got greedy. I could translate the whole drama, I said, and maybe even publish it. But I needed help. So I turned to my research assistant, Vikas, who lived in Varanasi and had never met Ghura Paul.

Vikas recognized the song immediately. It was from a famous drama about a group of villagers visiting a temple to a Hindu goddess. In the drama, Ghura Paul had made the key characters Catholic, and changed the temple to a Catholic shrine. But everything else was essentially the same—even the melody of the song.

Vikas said to me, in coarser Hindi than I care to translate, that Ghura Paul was making a fool of me.

I didn't confront Ghura Paul about the drama, but I did review every single song he had sung for me, every single poem he'd recited, and consulted experts on North Indian village customs. Apart from the drama, though, everything he'd sung or recited for me seemed to be exactly what he said it was—either an original composition or a Christian version of a Hindu devotional song, well known in the area.

The research seemed intact, but my relationship with Ghura Paul certainly wasn't.

When it came to providing funds for the operation, I felt constrained by rules set by the Indian government, and by the foundation providing my fellowship, that prohibited giving money to Indian nationals, except those I was actually employing for my research. And so, the easiest way to access funds for Ghura Paul's operation was for me to produce fake receipts, to lie and violate the law.

But the questions of propriety and legality soon gave way to another question that I angrily asked aloud when no one else was listening: Wasn't my interest in his life enough? I was a scholar, not a social worker, and Ghura Paul was trying to dupe me. There was no way I could or should provide an operation given the way he behaved.

My anger told me the situation was simple enough.

But once my anger cooled, I could see that maybe things weren't so simple. I did have more money than I could ever use—my fellowship gave me enough to live up to an American standard in an area where most people didn't have access to clean drinking water or electricity. American graduate students usually don't think of themselves as privileged, but my privilege was undeniable. And the research I was doing with Ghura Paul wasn't just about "knowledge" in some sort of abstract sense—it was going to get me a degree and a job.

I had to admit that Ghura Paul did have a claim on me. But even then, I didn't know how to weigh that claim in relation to all the legitimate claims for mercy among a community that was so poor and needy. Even with all that poverty and need, it was only Ghura Paul who was scheming to get something from me. So, I was back to the question of who "deserved" what. I could see that I had an obligation, but where that obligation lay wasn't clear to me. But it was clear to me that I wasn't free—either ethically or practically—to do whatever I saw fit.

It occurred to me that if I decided to give something back—to Ghura Paul, to the community, to the mission—perhaps the best way would be through some anonymous or hidden means. That was not because that route was more honorable, or more Christian—though it very well might be—but because it would be "free," free from the chain reaction and ensuing social repercussions that Father Sanchit feared would engulf the mission—and me.

***

I didn't share my labored thoughts with Ghura Paul. I didn't feel as though I could. I told him instead that my student status meant that I could not provide for his operation—something that was true in a strict sense, but was certainly far from the whole story.

He seemed to go along with what I said. But he still retained hope. One time he even had me write a letter to Pope John Paul II in Hindi about his operation. I did so, and sent the letter along with an English translation.

Ghura Paul lived with his wife, son, and daughter-in-law, though they did not seem to associate with him. His home had its own hand pump, so there were always people from the village who would come to fill water jugs—but they would rarely say anything to him.

He and I would typically just talk by ourselves. He usually called me "Brother," in English, a term that reflected that I was someone different from a priest, but also not just a student.

Toward the end of my time in India, I took Ghura Paul to Easter Mass at the mission. The provincial from the Indian Missionary Society was there. He had been a priest at the mission several decades earlier and knew Ghura Paul from those days. His name was Prem Annand, "the bliss of love."

I led Ghura Paul to Father Prem Annand, who was standing next to Father Sanchit on the veranda of the mission's rectory.

Ghura Paul's voice seemed softer than usual: "Father Prem Annand, you are a good shepherd. I need an operation to get my eyesight back."

Father Prem Annand clasped Ghura Paul's hand and then there was some back and forth in Hindi. Father Prem Annand then spoke with Father Sanchit in Malayalam, a South Indian language that neither Ghura Paul nor I understood, which is probably why he used it. After a few minutes, Father Prem Annand talked with Ghura Paul in Hindi and promised that the Indian Missionary Society would make sure that the operation would be done.

What I know about what transpired next is from a series of letters that Father Sanchit sent to me after I returned to the United States.

Father Prem Annand did keep his promise to pursue an operation, but it was never to be.

Upon examination, an ophthalmologist said that nothing could be done to restore Ghura Paul's eyesight. If he had been experiencing the sensation of light, it was something residual from the few nerve endings that remained intact—the eyes themselves were beyond treatment.

In the ensuing months, Ghura Paul's wife died, as did his daughter-in-law. Then he himself died of dysentery.

Maybe Ghura Paul's death was a mercy given that situation, but tragedy was the word that came to my mind when I read the news. For Ghura Paul, it must have seemed a cruel fate to finally be promised an operation only to learn that it could not be done.

***

Ghura Paul's baptismal namesake went blind. Acts 4:1-19 tells how Saul was in darkness for three days after his sight was taken on the road to Damascus as he heard Jesus' voice ask him, "Saul, Saul, why do you persecute me?" Ananias was commanded by God in a vision to lay hands upon Saul, but Ananias resisted, knowing how much Saul had done to persecute Christians. But Ananias finally did lay his hands upon Saul, and Saul became Paul, after the scales fell from his eyes.

Most people didn't want to touch Ghura Paul. But I laid hands on him: I helped him bathe, I led him to the bathroom, I washed his clothes. Priests laid hands upon him as well—during confession, and during charismatic prayer services devoted to healing. Mercy enough for Ghura Paul, we thought—mercy enough to make the scales fall from Ghura Paul's eyes so that he could "see" himself as a sinner.

But Ghura Paul wanted to see with physical eyes, not spiritual ones. And he laid hands upon us too, with pride and desperation. Maybe he sensed that what was going on was not really about mercy, but was instead a give and take, an exchange in which everyone would get something. I would get information for my research; the mission would get a high-profile, healed, Catholic; and he would get his eyesight back.

It's easy enough to say that Ghura Paul should have been open to receiving mercy without conditions—even what we would seek were we in his position: restored eyesight, an end to blindness. But it was Father Prem Annand who taught me that *giving* mercy needs to be without condition as well. We only truly open ourselves to giving mercy when we act without the harsh judgment that mercy is somehow undeserved. Mercy is powerful precisely because it's free.

Suggested Questions for Discussion
1. If Ghura Paul had asked you to pay for his operation, how would you have responded? Why?
2. Are some people more worthy of mercy than others? If so, why? If not, why not?
3. When someone asks us for something, what questions do we ask? What expectations do we have?
4. When have freedom and mercy been related in your life?

Suggested Questions for Private Reflection
1. Have you ever been merciful to someone and been disappointed by the results? Why were you disappointed—what did you expect?
2. Have you ever asked someone for something that you honestly needed? Were you treated mercifully?

Chapter Six

Mercy and Dignity

Slowly, deliberately, he unwrapped his bandage and I could see that most of the bandage was stuffed in a hole on the side of his foot.

On my first full day at the Ave Maria home for leprosy patients, I was shadowing two French nurses, Brigitte and Aimée.[1] Joining me were students from the College of the Holy Cross, who were preparing for their internship during their 2015 "Maymester" in India.

Ave Maria was clean, though the bright blue paint and whitewash on the walls could have used some touching up. Our sandals and flip-flops echoed through the halls. The windows were open and we could hear geese and emus honking and humming.

We followed Brigitte and Aimée into a room with two sets of steel bunks. On the polished stone floor was a mattress. Mr. Prakash sat on the mattress—the rest of his family were using the bunks.

Bollywood film music was playing from a radio at medium volume.

Mr. Prakash couldn't walk: both his feet were heavily bandaged, and he had lost most of his toes. Brigitte and Aimée approached him, and the students followed.

I hung back in the doorway.

Brigitte and Aimée put their hands on Mr. Prakash's shoulders and asked in Kannada—the local language—how he was doing. Mr. Prakash motioned to his buttocks and to the back of his legs: they were marked by deep sores and blisters.

Brigitte faced the students and pointed to Mr. Prakash. "He can't walk—you understand? He moves by pulling himself on the ground." The students nodded and took notes.

Brigitte and Aimée asked Mr. Prakash to roll over so they could tend to his wounds. The students inched closer, and Brigitte and Aimée used filtered water to clean the sores and blisters, and then applied salve and bandages.

I hadn't moved from my position by the door.

A Bollywood song came on that I recognized: "This joyful evening," a duet between two lovers.[2] It was a happy song, the harmonium, along with the *tabla*, gave it a bouncy lilt. The chorus began, "This joyful evening—it intoxicates me, a rope pulls me toward you."

I thought about the weird disjunction of hearing a Bollywood love song playing while someone was being treated for leprosy.

I thought I was part of the disjunction, too.

Maybe I shouldn't be there at all. Mr. Prakash deserved his privacy.

Brigitte and Aimée were doing their jobs; the students were new to India, so their curiosity was understandable.

But what about me? Should I enter the room or stay back?

I wasn't sure what to do. I wasn't sure because I wasn't sure how mercy and dignity fit together at Ave Maria. I had always thought about dignity as what you see when you look for the best in someone—the best part of their humanity. At the very least, it seemed as though I wouldn't be seeing Mr. Prakash at his best if I entered his room.

I entered the room anyway.

I stood behind the students and members of Mr. Prakash's family who were watching Brigitte and Aimée doing what they always did: being merciful.

***

The Ave Maria home is part of the Sumanahalli Society. Sumanahalli literally means "village of good-hearted people," and the

Sumanahalli campus is sixty-three acres of green on the edge of Bangalore, a cosmopolitan and rapidly expanding city in the South Indian state of Karnataka.[3] Sumanahalli is a Catholic organization that was founded in 1976 when the chief minister of Karnataka asked the Archdiocese of Bangalore to establish a leprosarium, since, in the chief minister's words, "It may be difficult for a government organization to provide this, as tasks of mercy are not generally effectively done by a bureaucratic system."[4]

Over the years, Sumanahalli's mission of mercy has grown beyond caring for leprosy-affected persons. There is now a treatment center for those suffering from HIV/AIDS as well as children left orphaned by the disease. The ministry also sponsors outreach programs for juvenile offenders and street children. The campus itself has approximately 380 residents, but its programs reach tens of thousands of people throughout South India every year.

Sumanahalli's approach to leprosy and HIV/AIDS is holistic, and it combines both corporal and spiritual works of mercy. Medical treatment, including reconstructive surgery, is provided free of charge, and there are quarters on the campus for patients' families as well. But the goal is not to "warehouse" patients; it is to reintegrate them into society. Sumanahalli builds homes, has had success in finding patients employment in government jobs, and also provides training in marketable crafts such as leatherwork, carpentry, and welding.

Father Peter D'Souza, the director, often describes those who come to Sumanahalli as "the poorest of the poor," and by this he intends no hyperbole. They are indeed poor economically: many are migrant laborers who get by on construction jobs—they have few resources and live in shantytowns or squatter colonies throughout Bangalore. They are also impoverished in other ways. Tremendous stigmas associated with both leprosy and HIV/AIDS exist in Indian society. "Leper" itself is a derogatory term in many Indian languages, and those suffering from leprosy are usually thrown out of their villages and often disowned by their families.

HIV/AIDS affected people face similar discrimination.

***

The leprosy bacillus attacks the nerve endings, damaging and finally destroying them. Because leprosy patients lose sensation in infected parts of the body, injuries and infections go unnoticed and untreated until they become so serious that amputation is the only option. The therapy for leprosy involves a strict regimen of drugs, administered over a period of six months to a year. The result of successful leprosy treatment is not the removal of pain, but its return. For leprosy patients, pain is a paradoxical mercy: it is a way to reestablish a relationship with one's physical self—a physical self that is otherwise numb, other, unfeeling.

The day after the students and I shadowed Brigitte and Aimée, I was walking through Ave Maria once again—this time by myself. In the TV room, patients were watching a version of the great Hindu epic *The Mahabharata*. Others were playing chess or talking quietly.

As I was walking, a gentleman motioned to me to come into his room. Heavyset, with white hair and a moustache, the gentleman wore a long white cloth with a red and gold border around his waist—he was bare-chested because of the Indian summer heat.

I went into his room, and he graciously offered me a chair. He sat down on his cot and pulled up another chair for his leg, which was heavily bandaged.

Slowly, deliberately, he unwrapped his bandage, and I could see that most of the bandage was stuffed in a hole on the side of his foot. He proceeded to remove the bandaging—it came out in reams, at a length of twelve inches or more. The gentleman then took out what appeared to be an awl with a plastic blue handle. He motioned with the awl toward the hole in his foot and shrugged his shoulders.

I understood. He had intentionally inflicted the wound with

the awl—trying to feel something, anything. It was an act that communicated the painless suffering of leprosy in a way that words could not.

I met the white-haired gentleman the next day when he asked me to sit next to him during a prayer service. There was a candle and all of us were arranged in a circle around it. Aimée led the service. She held a booklet of prayers in one hand and a rosary in the other.

Mr. Prakash was sitting on the ground, and he stretched out his hands in prayer—a gesture that everyone else in the circle mirrored. It was a charismatic form of prayer, focused on healing and receiving "Pentecostal" gifts such as speaking in tongues and prophecy.

While there was no speaking in tongues—at least from what I observed—I was struck by how appropriate that form of prayer is in that context.

Residents were holding out their hands—hands that had been mangled by disease. But those physical deformities did not diminish their dignity or their personhood.

Central to charismatic forms of prayer is touching and being touched—and often these prayer services involved the laying on of hands, not just by priests and lay healers, but also by the residents themselves.

Leprosy is contagious, but only after prolonged exposure in unhygienic conditions—in any case, the leprosy bacillus is usually passed by nasal droplets, not by touch. But leprosy-affected persons—often identifiable by their sores and lesions—are considered to be immediate sources of physical and moral contagion.

When leprosy-affected persons touch and are touched—just as when they feel pain—it is a mercy that affirms their dignity: they are full and whole human beings, not objects of fear or disgust.

***

The Sumanahalli campus is bordered by a road that teems with speeding motorcycles, automobiles, and buses. There's also a concrete overpass, a flyover, that gives the growing urban sprawl a vertical dimension. If you manage to cross the road safely and avoid the cows napping under the flyover, you'll see greenery again and the gate of the hostel for HIV/AIDS patients and their families. Taking a right turn around and behind the hostel brings you to a grove of palm trees that opens up to the precincts of St. Joseph's Convent School where children from the main Sumanahalli campus and local squatter communities study.

Over a two-week period, I joined Holy Cross students in teaching classes at St. Joseph's. Each one of us had our own class, ranging from "first standard" to "tenth standard," to use the Indian way to refer to what in America we call "grades" or "years." The Holy Cross students shared whatever they could to encourage St. Joseph's students to practice their English skills. Margo did vigorous versions of "Head, Shoulders, Knees and Toes." Rob tried to get his students to count up to a million. Carrie did "Row, Row, Row Your Boat," and Cristi played "Simon Says" and drew a hopscotch pattern on the dirt field. Maria played volleyball with her students, and Paula showed photos of her family and friends to explain what life was like in America.

I was the substitute Hindi teacher: Hindi is a North Indian language that is not spoken very widely in South India, so it's part of the curriculum as a secondary or tertiary language, along with English.

I had hoped that my status as the "foreign professor" might insulate me from the normal shenanigans that substitute teachers experience. But on my first day I immediately had to break up fights and deal with obviously less than urgent requests for bathroom breaks. It was almost impossible for me to keep the students quiet enough so that we could begin to recite the Hindi poem that was supposed to occupy us for the rest of the day.

After a while I gave up on the official lesson plan and tried talking to the students about life in America. Later on, I pulled out my camera and let students take pictures with it: I was the test subject for showing off their photographic skills. Students took multiple pictures of me standing next to them. I have a funny look on my face—a kind of half-grin with a deer in the headlights look, a distinctly undignified posture for a college professor. I'm wearing jeans and a T-shirt soaked in sweat from the summer heat.

But the students are holding onto me tightly—with both hands.

After that first day in the classroom, I carried my aching body out of the school and started making my way back to the Sumanahalli campus. I walked through a dusty field where there were students playing cricket and volleyball. A young girl ran up behind me, shouting—in English—"brother!"

She came up beside me and introduced herself in Hindi: "My name is Sharmila."

"My name is Mathew. Where did you learn Hindi?"

Sharmila explained that she came from a town near Mumbai, in the state of Maharashtra.

"May I walk with you, brother?" she asked.

"Yes, of course." I held out my hand.

And we walked.

Sharmila was dressed in her school uniform: a navy-blue frock, white button-up shirt, white ankle socks, and black shoes with a buckle. She looked about twelve, the same age as my youngest daughter, Joy, but she was a little shorter, just under five feet tall.

Sharmila peppered me with questions: "Is it cold where you live? What do you eat? Are you married? What are the names of your children? What do you think of Obama?"

I didn't have the opportunity to balance things out by asking questions of my own.

After about ten minutes, we came to the road. I turned left to go up to Ave Maria and the rest of the Sumanahalli campus.

Sharmila turned right and entered the home for HIV/AIDS-affected persons and their families.

I saw Sharmila each day after that, but I never inquired about how HIV/AIDS had impacted her life. Maybe a conversation about that would have been an act of mercy for Sharmila by breaking through the stigma attached to those affected by the disease. But such a discussion might have made her feel that her dignity was now in jeopardy.

The relationship between mercy and dignity often depends on the context. While the craziness of St. Joseph's School might seem a long way from mercy and dignity as conventionally understood, the school did strike me as being a place of mercy and dignity precisely because being seen and treated as a student—in need of both education and discipline—is obviously qualitatively different from being treated as an outcaste or being reminded that one's status is somehow "different" or "special."

Privacy protects someone in a context where certain kinds people are seen not just as "undignified" but also as not worthy of dignity in the first place. An assumption of privacy also goes along with an appreciation of human dignity: it respects an individual's own ability to define herself or himself as long as it does not negatively impact someone or something else. Sharmila did not volunteer anything to me about how HIV/AIDS had changed her life with her family. My honest sense was that she just wanted to be a kid with me.

Sometimes mercy comes by directly confronting the ideas and practices that devalue human beings. At St. Joseph's School, I saw how mercy can also come in another way—by simply assuming someone's personhood rather than ostentatiously drawing attention to it in a way that unwittingly gives even more power to existing prejudices.

**

In his encyclical *Evangelium Vitae*, "The Gospel of Life," St. John Paul II reminds us of one of the central tenets of Christianity: Human beings are made in the likeness of God, the product of a special decision God has made to establish a "particular and specific bond."[5] Indeed, as *Evangelium Vitae* argues, "whether man or woman, there is a reflection of God himself, the definitive goal and fulfillment of every human person."[6]

To see and treat another person as a reflection of God is to understand that a special relationship with God is made possible through, with, and in that person—at that time, in that very moment. Human dignity is relational: it proceeds vertically from God, but also moves horizontally to connect us all. Mercy that respects human dignity affirms not just the special bond between humans and God, but also the special bond that humans share with one another.

Mr. Prakash's condition was visible to all, and so I probably sensed that not entering his room would have been taken as a sign of fear and rejection. In retrospect, I think my concern about Mr. Prakash's dignity was a concern about relationality: I hadn't been introduced to him and felt as though there was simply nothing for me to do. Brigitte and Aimée certainly didn't need my help, not even with mundane tasks like holding bandages or disposing of cotton swabs, which were the only things that I could have helped with anyway.

But I entered the room. I entered, a familiar Bollywood song playing all the while, with a male voice singing: "This joyful evening, it intoxicates me. A rope pulls me toward you."

I started humming along with the song. Then I repeated, softly, the chorus, and was joined by relatives that had gathered around Mr. Prakash.

Whether my singing was an act of mercy, I cannot say, though I must admit that I'm not particularly good with songs in any language. But singing does bring people together—in any language, and at any place—and it is something that is easy enough to do, as long as one isn't unduly concerned about one's own "dignity" in the sense of being aloof or somehow beyond the rough and tumble of ordinary life.

***

In thinking about Mr. Prakash and the work of Sumanahalli, I'm reminded of the words of Mother Teresa that I read when I first went to India: "Think of the poor as Jesus in disguise."

I got the point then, and I get the point now: look beyond the pathetic external appearance to see the dignity within.

But when I reflect more deeply on Mr. Prakash and the work of Sumanahalli, there is another phrase that seems more appropriate. It's actually a line from St. Ignatius of Loyola's favorite prayer, the *Anima Christi*: "O good Jesus, hear me. Within thy wounds, hide me. Separated from Thee, let me never be."[7]

The wounds of Christ are points where Jesus' own woundedness opens up to let us in—and it is in and through Jesus' wounds that we can experience God's merciful love for all of us. At Sumanahalli, leprosy-affected persons aren't simply "Jesus in disguise," *they are Jesus*. They have dignity not in spite of their wounds but because of them.

The Bollywood song changed to a more recent one that I didn't know. Brigitte and Aimée finished treating Mr. Prakash, and the students and I said goodbye for the time being and slowly walked out of the room.

I thanked Mr. Prakash by folding my hands together in front of my chest and by bowing slightly, which is a traditional Indian form of showing respect. I then gently touched his shoulder. In all that I thought and felt about mercy and dignity in Mr. Prakash's presence, there was something basic and important that I forgot to do.

I did not ask his name.

I use the name Mr. Prakash now as a kind of placeholder—as a reminder to myself that even though I did not learn his real name, he most certainly was not nameless.

Suggested Questions for Discussion

1. Would you have entered Mr. Prakash's room? In your view, what issues would be involved?

2. When you think of people being treated with dignity, what examples come to mind?

3. What questions can we ask ourselves to make sure we are being merciful and respecting someone else's dignity?

4. Has pain ever been a mercy in your life? In the lives of those around you?

Suggested Questions for Private Reflection

1. Are there particular kinds of people that you shy away from? Why?

2. In what ways could you bring mercy to someone whom you might ordinarily reject or ignore?

Chapter Seven

Mercy and Kindness

I needed to look past—or see in a more complex way—the initially off-putting aspects of Dieter, such as his aggressive evangelization for Jehovah's Witnesses or his childhood in Nazi Germany.

The blue Mazda always made throaty sounds. It had a rotary engine that sounded like a hot rod revving when I pressed down the clutch and gunned the gas.

But the noise I was hearing was different. It was a grinding and grating coming from the rear wheels, not the engine.

I got nervous for a moment: It was the parish's car and I was the parish assistant. I was responsible. But I knew Dieter would help me out, even though he wasn't a member of the parish. Dieter was trained as a Volkswagen mechanic, and he was the only one in a hundred-mile radius who knew anything about foreign cars. Luckily, his house wasn't as far as the Piggly Wiggly where I was heading to pick up some groceries.

Dieter lived in a small development, where lawns had to fight against incursions of sand and sagebrush. I pulled the Mazda under the carport, right beside his blue Volkswagen bus.

Dieter came out and stood on the steps leading from his home. He was well dressed as usual: gray double-knit pants, a checkered dress shirt, and black lace-up shoes. His salt-and-pepper hair was trimmed acutely over his ears and parted on the right side with a slight hint of a wave. He offered a mock salute and a smile.

"What can I do for you, there, Mat?"

I explained the noise coming from the rear wheels.

"Sounds kind of Mickey Mouse to me," Dieter said with a glint in his eye.

"Mickey Mouse" was Dieter's favorite adjective. It meant everything from cheap and poorly made to a cartoonish fantasy. I had no idea where the phrase came from. I hadn't heard it before and have never heard it from anyone since. Whenever Dieter would say "Mickey Mouse," his German accent would come through as he'd lengthen and harden the "ou" and the "s" in "Mouse": "Mowze."

"Let me check for it you, there, Mat." Dieter got out a dolly from the shed at the end of the driveway and pulled himself under the Mazda.

I heard the twist of a ratchet, metal scraping, and a pop.

"Definitely Mickey Mouse!" Dieter said as he pulled himself out and sat there on the dolly. He held out a large pebble between his thumb and index finger. "That is where the sound was coming from, there, Mat. You had this in your wheel well."

I was relieved. "What do I owe you?" I asked jokingly.

"Oh, I'll send the bill to the Holy See," Dieter laughed and slapped me on the back. "Since you're here, let's have a beer and play some pool."

The Piggly Wiggly could wait, I decided.

***

It was 1982 and I was living in the Southwest. I had decided to take a gap year between high school and college. A rural Catholic parish had been kind enough to accept me as volunteer, and I lived at the rectory.

Over my time in the Southwest I had gotten used to kindnesses: people were friendly, so friendly that there was even the custom of waving to passing cars on the back roads even when you didn't recognize the person who was driving. People always seemed to be looking out for one another.

Dieter helping me with the car was not an uncommon kindness in that context. But my relationship with Dieter did strike me as being uncommonly kind. Dieter reached out to me, a teenager, when I was a long way from home.

Kindness isn't mercy—not exactly, anyway—but mercy and kindness are related. I think of kindness as something thoughtful or helpful. Kindness strikes me as merciful when it comes unexpectedly, from a surprising source—from someone like Dieter.

***

Kindness was about the furthest thing from my mind after about a half-hour into my first visit to Dieter's home. In fact, I was trying to find an excuse to leave and never come back.

Dieter had already explained the basics to me: only 144,000 would go to heaven to rule with Christ, the rest would live on an earth that had been cleansed. The end was coming soon—within a generation that saw the events of 1914, the Great War that marked Satan's last effort to challenge Jehovah God. Only members of Jehovah God's theocratic organization, Jehovah's Witnesses, would remain when God's kingdom came to Earth.

Dieter and I were on the town's adult soccer team, and he and I were the only ones who knew anything about how soccer was really played—European style. After one game, when all of us on the team were helping ourselves to silver cans of Coors Light, I heard someone playfully ask Dieter whether he had stashed *Awake!* magazines in the cooler.

That Dieter was a Jehovah's Witness made me curious, and when I asked him about it, he immediately invited me over for a discussion at his home.

So, one day later, there we were sitting face-to-face in canvas director's chairs in his photography studio. Dieter did custodial work by night and photography by day. It struck me as rather incongruous when I spotted books about Yousuf Karsh and other famous photographers under copies of *The Watchtower* on Dieter's desk.

"How about I show you some photos, there, Mat?" he said.

I was relieved that Dieter was dropping his Jehovah's Witnesses pitch to show me some of his work. I was expecting wedding or graduation photos.

But the pictures Dieter held out looked old: they were black and white, about three or four inches wide, and framed by a white border.

The first picture had Catholic bishops, front and center, making the Nazi salute.

The second picture showed what appeared to be another group of bishops, with aspergilla in their hands to sprinkle holy water. Artillery pieces were lined up to be blessed under a Nazi flag.

"Hitler was a Catholic, you know," Dieter said.

"Well, if he was, I'm sure Hitler was excommunicated. Nazism was pagan," I said, trying to hold my ground.

"I was in the Hitler Youth—the *Deutsches Jungvolk*," Dieter admitted. "I didn't know better. Now I think it was all kind of 'Mickey Mouse.'"

Hitler, Nazi flags, Catholic bishops, Mickey Mouse—too many confusing images for me.

I started to squirm in the director's chair. I remember it making squeaking sounds on the hardwood floor.

Then Dieter suddenly said: "Okay, enough about religion and politics. Let's have a beer."

***

Dieter and I withdrew from the photography studio and made our way to the countertop island that set off the small kitchen from the living room where a pool table took up most of the space. He got me a mug from the freezer and expertly poured the beer so it had a nice frothy head.

I was looking forward to the brief alcohol kick—a kick that

might give me the confidence to propel myself out of there.

"Know how to play pool?" Dieter asked me as I was shifting my beer mug from hand to hand since it was so cold.

"Well, not really," I said, "but my parents bought me a pocket billiards table for Christmas when I was nine years old."

"We Jehovah's Witnesses don't celebrate Christmas, there, Mat. It's a pagan holiday."

I had finished my beer and was overcome with a desire for another. I figured I'd stay for a bit.

"Can you teach me to play?" I asked.

"Why yes, there, Mat—I can teach you. It won't be Mickey Mouse coming from me."

Dieter was right about it not being Mickey Mouse—he gave me a full lesson. He taught me how to rack and explained the differences between the games of eight ball and nine ball. He showed me various ways to hold the cue: cradling it between my thumb and index finger; using my knuckles as a groove or my middle finger as a semicircular brace. He also demonstrated the differences between backspin and topspin, and impressed upon me the importance of considering the "leave" of the cue ball and the setup for the next shot.

We practiced and played for the whole afternoon—racking and shooting, and sipping beer.

Dieter's children came home from school—all six of them. They spread out in the living room and the photography studio and did their homework for an hour or so. Then Dieter's eldest daughter, Esther, set down her books to get dinner ready: pork chops, canned corn, biscuits and gravy on the side.

Everyone lined up, eldest to youngest, and served themselves from the countertop island where Esther had set out the food on big serving platters and in bowls.

We all then crowded into the living room and ate as we watched a PBS documentary on Hawaii. The television was mounted on the wall since the pool table took up so much room. A shot of a waterfall came on, and the camera lingered on the mist refracting the sun's rays over purple orchids and fern-covered stones.

"Jehovah's creation is sure beautiful," Dieter said.

***

That dinner was the first of many for me at Dieter's home. The dinners weren't fancy and sometimes they were crowded and rushed. But I appreciated the homey feeling, the sense of being connected to a family when mine was so far away.

Dieter recognized and respected that family connection. One time, a couple of months into my stay in the Southwest, we were sitting once again in the director's chairs in his studio. The Catholic Nazi pictures had been safely put away—he only showed them to me that one time, in fact—and much of the Jehovah's Witnesses talk had receded into the background of our friendship.

Dieter leaned forward in his chair and lifted his beer mug to toast me.

"You know, Mat, your foster parents have raised you well." If Dieter's real intent in showing me kindness had been to convert me, he would have focused on undermining the relationship I had with my parents instead of praising it.

"I'm a fortunate guy," I said.

"You know, there, Mat," Dieter reflected, "there are three types of people: people who talk about things; people who talk about other people; people who talk about ideas. You talk about ideas, there, Mat."

Dieter and I did talk about ideas. Usually, we talked about culture: German culture, sometimes, but more often we'd focus on trying to put our fingers on how and why culture in the Southwest was different. Dieter was from Europe; I was from the Northeast. We shared an outsider status. Down deeper, we shared an emotional vulnerability—a need—that drew us together in that time and place.

"You know, there, Mat, it's hard not having a wife around.

When Vicky died last year, I thought it was a kind of Mickey Mouse situation with me and all my kids. I'm a widower. It's nice to have someone different to talk to."

Dieter letting down his guard? Revealing something of the struggles he was facing as a single father? I knew that every week must have brought new challenges with only the custodial work and the photography for income.

One time I tried to reciprocate his hospitality in a small way by buying presents for him and his family. It was two weeks into January, so I figured it would be beyond the statute of limitations for Christmas gift giving. Dieter graciously accepted the gifts with the comment, "Well, there, Mat, none of us need a holiday to give each other presents." A couple of weeks later, he gifted me a book about the history of billiards.

I felt that Dieter and I were like close relatives, sort of like an uncle and nephew or elder and younger brother. His place was home for me. Whenever I mentioned that I felt I was overstaying my welcome, or eating more of Esther's cooking than I should, Dieter would say, "Oh, Mat, there are so many of us that one more person don't matter."

Fate, or providence, did intervene to balance things out. Toward the end of my stay in the Southwest, Dieter won a meat raffle at Piggly Wiggly that gave his family enough steak and pork chops for several months of dinners.

"Jehovah always provides," Dieter said to me when he told me the news.

***

When I left the Southwest and entered Amherst College, I kept in contact with Dieter and he invited me down over my freshman year winter break. He drove four hours to the nearest airport to pick me up when I flew in from the Northeast. And we did pick up where we left off—his kids were a little older, and some were thinking about full-time missionary work as Jehovah's Witnesses, but the family feeling was comfortably the same. I bunked with his two oldest sons for about a week and played a lot of pool.

The next year, when I was a sophomore, I bought my ticket for a winter break visit and called Dieter.

"I went and got myself married," Dieter told me excitedly right after I said "hello."

I was taken aback, but I offered my congratulations. I thought the wedding must have been preceded by a very short engagement.

When I told him about my travel plans, Dieter was silent for a moment and then said, "I'm not sure we have room enough for you, there, Mat."

I knew other people in the area—I did have other friends that I could stay with—but I wanted to stay with Dieter. He was family—and I got a little pushy.

I told Dieter that I wanted to meet his wife.

"Well, okay then, there, Mat. I'll come get you at the airport," Dieter said—leaving it open as to whether I could stay with him.

Dieter did drive four hours in his Volkswagen bus to pick me up. His wife was with him—she sat in the front seat and held Dieter's hand while I spread out in the back.

When we arrived at Dieter's home, the kids were out at school.

"Welcome back, Mat," Dieter said after I had deposited my suitcase near the pool table.

"You can rest a while before you make other arrangements," he said.

I had already prepared for this eventuality by contacting other friends before I came down. I called my former supervisor at the local food bank and she promised to come pick me up.

I actually don't remember how I said goodbye to Dieter. I just have an image of him standing arm in arm with his wife by the door—looking happy and complete.

I grabbed my suitcase and walked out the door, under the

carport, and into a waiting car.

***

It's common and understandable to think of mercy in terms of big things—acts of forgiveness, sacrifice, or understanding. But mercy is also revealed in the little things, in the small kindnesses we show to one another. Thinking about mercy in terms of little things can be helpful when big things seemingly get in the way—things like religion, race, language, and class.

Kindness is indeed a mercy when it comes from an unexpected source.

I don't know why Dieter suddenly changed topics during our first meeting—why he put away the photographs of the Nazi bishops and got me a beer instead. But maybe he sensed my own vulnerability and fear and decided to back off. Face-to-face with a real-live Catholic, maybe Dieter realized that the stereotypes and the prejudices didn't fit very well. From my side, I needed to look past—or see in a more complex way—the initially off-putting aspects of Dieter, such as his aggressive evangelization for Jehovah's Witnesses or his childhood in Nazi Germany. Though Dieter and I had different religious beliefs, we shared many of the same values. We also had families, we had both experienced joy and pain in our families, and we both liked to play pool and drink beer.

But I still ended my friendship with Dieter when I left his home that day. I was hurt; I never contacted him again. I failed to recognize that my own behavior—buying a ticket without consulting him first and assuming a closer, more familial relationship than in fact existed—set me up for what I perceived as rejection. I didn't even appreciate that Dieter and his wife drove all that way to pick me up at the airport. I was young, impulsive, needy—I would heedlessly and tenaciously hang on to someone long after a relationship had completed its natural course.

While Dieter had been a widower and was needy, too, his family situation had changed in a way that didn't—that couldn't—include me as it once did. I suppose some kind of messy ending was inevitable given the unstable dynamic that vulnerability created between us.

I teach a class about Jehovah's Witnesses now and one thing I am sure to do is share my experiences with Dieter—experiences that taught me about the complex human side of a religious movement that is all too often seen in terms of suspicion and fear. But in my more private movements, I try to think through what my friendship with Dieter taught me about the possibility and perils of kindness and vulnerability. Experiencing kindness in the moment, as I did so many times in Dieter's home, can be a prelude to an unkind ending if we're not aware of our own vulnerabilities. Once we realize and accept how kindness and vulnerability connect all of us in hidden and powerful ways, we can be open to experiences that we would have never thought possible. Dieter and I—a Jehovah's Witness and a Roman Catholic—became friends. We didn't need to agree on theology for that to happen. We just needed to accept how much we needed mercy.

Suggested Questions for Discussion
1. This story talks about mercy in relation to vulnerability and fear. Where do you see those connections in this chapter?
2. Can you share an experience of kindness that came from an unexpected source and impacted you in a surprising way?
3. What are some of the little things you have done to connect with people whom you saw as distant or different?
4. How do we know when kindness is sincere and when it has an ulterior motive? Or is it impossible to know?

Suggested Questions for Private Reflection
1. What vulnerabilities do you have? How do they relate to how you experience and express kindness?
2. Have you ever been afraid of showing kindness to someone because you weren't sure how it would be received?

Chapter Eight

Mercy and Truth

I'm not sure whether it added up, but at the time I recalled a line from Dostoyevsky, often quoted by Dorothy Day, the co-founder of the Catholic Worker movement: "Love in action is harsh and dreadful when compared to love in dreams."

One evening, Ricky stood at the office door. He wore baggy blue jeans, white high-tops with a gray Nike swoosh, and a plain undershirt. Close-cropped hair, razor stubble on his chin, plain gold stud sparkling from his left earlobe.

Whenever I met with a resident in the downstairs office, I would remember that Sister Virginia was stabbed to death a few feet from where I was sitting.

I never knew Sister Virginia.

But I had been told that she was talking to a resident with the door closed when she was murdered. I thought that was good enough reason to fib a little in the interest of caution: "Come in, Ricky, just leave the door open, the radiator's acting up and it's too hot."

Ricky seated himself in the chair across the desk and leaned toward me.

I looked at him through piles of papers and folders. He was about half a foot shorter than I, but he could bench-press twice his weight—and therefore mine.

Ricky returned my polite look with a piercing stare, like a boxer facing down his opponent at the weigh-in before a fight.

I glanced to make sure the door was still open.

"I've been lying to you," Ricky said.

"Really? 'Bout what?" I asked.

"See this?" Ricky pointed to the scarred indentation on his deltoid. I remembered the intake interview when Ricky told me that he had been shot in a hold up.

"That didn't happen the way I said," Ricky began to explain. "I didn't get shot during a robbery at a convenience store—like I was an innocent bystander or something."

"What happened, then?" I said matter-of-factly.

"I got shot by the drug dealer I was working with. He owed me money, so I tried to take it."

"Why'd you lie to me?" I asked.

"I didn't think you'd accept me if I told the truth," Ricky explained.

Ricky might have been right about that, I had to admit. But it had been three months since Ricky arrived, and I was convinced that this was his breakthrough. Being able to talk truthfully about himself—and take responsibility for his actions—was obviously necessary if he ever wanted to turn his life around. I suppose his confession was a mercy too—an unexpected act of love and trust—especially since I didn't want what happened to Sister Virginia to happen to me or anyone else.

***

It was 1989 and Graced Opportunities had room for thirteen young men—thirteen otherwise homeless "residents" ripe for redemption. A transition from the streets to a normal life—that was the ministry as envisioned by Father Jim, who almost single-handedly persuaded his religious order to buy the South Bronx brownstone a decade earlier.

Father Jim didn't promise me money—though I would get ten dollars a week—but he did promise me the chance to rub against the hard edges of life. And that appealed to my "edgy" sense of self.

I remember the first time I went from Graced Opportunities to the local post office. I walked south along Willis Avenue and turned left down 141st Street, passing a lot where long crab grass grew around bricks and bottles, tires and trash. I hurried along the broken sidewalk, through some shaky shooters bargaining for dirty syringes, and past prostitutes hustling for late-afternoon business, their hollow cheeks pink with blush.

Rubbing against rough edges like that made me feel light and alive.

But smoothing down the rough edges of the residents—that made me feel like dead weight.

I wasn't the only one working at Graced Opportunities. We had a staff of volunteers who were dedicated and skilled: social workers in training, future seminarians, former residents who had come to give something back. I felt like the odd man out—college was a year behind me and I was just back from India and Pakistan.

Luckily for me, Father Jim had a strong devotion to St. Thérèse and her "little way." When he came every Sunday for dinner, we'd talk and he'd often have a St. Thérèse quote. The one I remember best is: "If every tiny flower wanted to be a rose, spring would lose its loveliness."[1] With my hulking six-foot-one-inch frame, I didn't make a very believable tiny flower, and blossoming into a rose was doubtful given my hygiene habits. But I did get what Father Jim was saying through St. Thérèse—mercy is in the little things.

***

For mercy's sake, I did a lot of little things during the eight months I was at Graced Opportunities.

After Francis was diagnosed with HIV/AIDS, I regularly cleaned the bathroom he used since everyone else was afraid to. I played chess with Pablo—he had come from El Salvador after his family was massacred right before his eyes. I took cooking lessons from Diego and Luis—they had been referred to us by a tourist agency in Times Square after they showed up from Puerto Rico and didn't know where else to go. I helped Roger practice for his driver's test in the red Chevy that had been given to us by a devout Catholic charismatic lady from Long Island. And I drug-tested Anthony—a Ghanaian immigrant who was thrown out by his relatives—and discharged him for smoking crack.

Ricky was the resident I was closest to. We'd talk about street culture: he'd share with me Afrika Bambaataa's latest licks or tell me about the gold "grills" he used to wear on his front teeth. Ricky's family was from Puerto Rico, and they had settled in Brooklyn—either Bushwick or Brownsville, but I couldn't remember exactly. Ricky was recommended by a social worker from the homeless shelter where he was staying, and that was good enough for me when he came for an intake interview.

***

Several weeks after his drug-dealing confession, Ricky confronted me again.

"You tell us this is our home, but you lock us out!" Ricky's jeans and jacket were soaked through from standing out in the winter rain.

"Father Ed's orders," I said. "It's tough love."

Ed had been posted to Graced Opportunities recently after a five-year hiatus from the priesthood. He was in recovery and had trained as an addictions counselor. He wanted the residents to look for jobs and made it clear that everyone had to be out by 8:00 a.m. and that they would not be let in until 4:00 p.m.

Ricky had decided to come back early, and I let him in when I saw him at the front door.

"Look," I said to Ricky, "you're not going to change your life just by sitting on the couch watching Regis Philbin in the mornings."

"But it's raining outside!" Ricky said, reiterating the obvious.

"You're young—you can manage," I added, though I was sympathetic. I let Ricky stay to dry off.

The next day, Ricky upped the ante: "I want you to help me find a job."

I was drinking Café Bustello after a breakfast of burned bacon and watery eggs. Ed had gone out early for a meeting with Father Jim in Brooklyn; we were understaffed and looking for more volunteers.

"Sure, Ricky," I said, trying to hide my nerves.

We went into the office.

"What about that fuel-oil company? I have experience working with a fuel-oil company."

"I told you to go there a couple of days ago!" I had given Ricky the name of an oil company that was looking for employees. I got it from a jobs' circular I picked up at the Safeway a couple of blocks away.

"Make the call," Ricky insisted.

So I called and asked for the owner. I introduced myself by saying that I had read his job posting and that I was calling from a "transitional home for young men."

"You mean a shelter? Isn't there a government program that could help me hire someone?" the owner asked.

"Not that I know of." I didn't have a follow-up. I had no idea what I was doing.

"Well, give me a call if you find about a government program. I'm sure there's one." The owner then hung up, politely.

"You see what I'm talking about," Ricky said. "You didn't even get to mentioning my name!"

Maybe Ricky did have experience with a fuel-oil company, but it had surely been off the books. In any case, few employers are inclined to show mercy to someone whose resume is a rap sheet.

"Sorry, I tried," I said as Ricky turned his back to me and stomped out of the office.

***

"What are we doing here, Ed?" I asked.

It was the following afternoon, and the residents were still out.

I was standing on the green carpet in the living room, the near-by bookcases crammed with self-help tracts and pamphlets about the secrets of Fátima. Father Ed had just come in from getting his brown Pontiac worked on. The battery had regularly been stolen until he put a chain under the hood, and someone had recently thrown a brick through the back windshield, perhaps in retaliation.

"Let's go to the office," he said. The office was downstairs, right next to the kitchen.

Ed was wearing jeans, a windbreaker, and a plaid flannel shirt, fraying at the cuffs. His wire-rim glasses were perched on his nose, and he hadn't shaved or had a haircut in a while.

"What are you talking about?" Ed sat down, took off his blue knit cap, and put his running shoes up on the desk.

I sat opposite him.

"We're supposed to be helping these guys, and we're not," I said.

"We're giving these guys structure. We're creating a context," Ed explained.

I let out a sigh and said, "We don't seem to be doing a very good job."

Ed raised his voice: "We give these guys a place to sleep, we give them hot meals, and we hold them accountable for living their lives."

"But, Ed, who are we accountable to? We obviously weren't accountable to Ricky—I couldn't get him a job. And we locked him out in the rain."

Ed paused before speaking again.

"Let me tell you something: You're not Ricky. Don't make his story yours; don't make his troubles yours. Give him the dignity of being his own person—not an extension of you."

Still, locking the residents out really did seem merciless to me. But Ed was big into personal boundaries—how they were necessary, especially when living in close quarters with people. He was a recovering addict himself and always said that addicts like to get messed up in other people's lives. Keeping a rigid structure was not just about forcing the residents to get on with their lives, it was about protecting us all from one another.

I'm not sure whether it added up, but at the time I recalled a line from Dostoyevsky, often quoted by Dorothy Day, the co-founder of the Catholic Worker movement: "Love in action is harsh and dreadful when compared to love in dreams."[2]

***

We continued with the 8:00 a.m. to 4:00 p.m. regimen.

One morning, Ricky didn't come down. I went upstairs to find him hacking and gasping for air.

"Oh, my…" I wasn't sure what to do.

"Gotta stay home today," Ricky said.

That made sense. Of course it made sense. I called down to Ed, and here he came, earnestly lumbering up the creaky stairs.

"Ricky, you okay?" Ed asked.

Ricky was lying on his side, a bed sheet by his mouth. He couldn't suck in enough air to speak.

Ed was quick. "Mat, get him to the hospital—now."

During the fifteen-minute drive to the hospital, I kept my eyes in front of me. Ricky's rasping was so loud I had to focus on the streetlights to keep my concentration.

Lincoln Medical and Mental Health Center was a brick megalith of perpendicular rectangles scored by vents, ducts, and rows of square windows. I pulled into the garage at 144th and Park Avenue. It was a straight-line walk to the emergency room.

Ricky needed to be stabilized. A nurse put him in a bed and gave him oxygen, and all the while he clutched my hand. "Thank you, thank you," he said in short bursts, fogging up the mask.

It took about an hour before Ricky was allowed to move.

There were processions down white corridors and through dingy checkpoints—all to fill out forms. Finally, we arrived in a respiratory specialist's waiting room. We picked a pair of plastic chairs next to the potted plastic plants. I helped Ricky sit.

He kept holding my hand.

A couple of hours passed and Ricky started bantering with the nurses at the station. Proof of his recovery came when he started whispering to me about how one of the nurses had a special glow and a sexy birthmark on her neck.

It had been about seven hours total when Ricky finally saw a doctor—he popped out of his chair quickly when his name was called. He came out of the doctor's office after only a few minutes, coughing mildly and holding a piece of paper, which he hastily put in his jeans' pocket.

We made it back to Graced Opportunities for dinner.

It was grilled cheese. We kept five-pound bricks stacked like bullion in a circa-1960 icebox with a swing handle. Ed had treated the brick like a Sunday ham and cut the slices thick. They didn't melt well.

Ricky made no complaint as he sat himself at the table with the rest of the residents. He slapped my back and kept repeating himself, calling me "a trooper," "a friend," "a good Christian."

After his fifth sandwich, Ricky let out an unlabored breath and said, "Time for Baywatch!"

The rest of the residents followed him upstairs to the living room.

Ed stayed behind while I got ready for cleanup.

"You know what you have to do, don't you?" Ed said to me.

"Yes, I do." I knew it had to be done before Ricky filled the prescription.

***

The next morning Ricky came downstairs, seemingly hale and well.

I asked him to go to the kitchen.

I had given a version of the speech many times before: "Ricky, we suspect you of illegal drug use. We have the right to administer a drug test to you. Refusal means immediate discharge. It's essential that you follow procedure so that the sample will be untainted. Now, please go to the bathroom. And leave the door open. Fill this up and give it to me."

Ricky nodded.

I gave him the plastic container.

Ricky faced me but immediately lowered his head. I thought he'd seized up with shame, but he unzipped his fly and filled the container after stopping a couple of times.

When Ricky handed me the sample, he confessed.

"The test is going to come back dirty. I smoked grass."

"We'll talk after the results come in," I said.

"Straight up—it was just grass," Ricky assured me, looking me straight in the eye.

The container was warm in my hands and made me want to retch. I quickly put it in an express mailing box to be sent to the lab. I walked it down to the post office myself.

***

I received the letter a couple of days later: "The results indicate opioids and benzoylecgonine."

Opioids were enough. I didn't know what benzoylecgonine was—but I figured it must be a byproduct of cocaine. I thought Ricky must have been speed-balling—combining heroin and cocaine and smoking it.

That stuff would burn your lungs from the inside out.

I talked to Ed and he made the call to a Catholic-run homeless shelter a few blocks north and reserved a bed there for Ricky.

Just before dinner, while everyone was watching television, we called Ricky down to the kitchen one last time.

Ed was matter-of-fact and measured. "Ricky, we're discharging you for illegal drug use," he said. "You'll be going to a shelter tonight."

Ed was standing about ten feet away from me, where the kitchen opened into a corridor by the office and up the stairs to the living room. I was in front of the sink, by the back door. Ricky was in between. This was our standard positioning for a discharge—there would be two clear escape routes for us. Sometimes residents got violent.

"Just for smoking grass?" Ricky was bold.

I said: "We're way, way, beyond that. You've been using heroin and cocaine."

Ricky went silent, and I motioned for him to go up the stairs. I followed him through the living room and up to the second floor where the residents slept. There were bunks, dressers, and old steam radiators.

Ricky put everything in a duffle—T-shirts, jeans, and a box cutter.

"Box cutter? That's against the rules too—give it to me," I demanded.

"Need to protect myself," Ricky explained, looking directly at me.

Then he turned away, chucking the box cutter on his bunk, and stormed down the stairs.

He stood there waiting for me at the door. I opened it, and he went out, down the steps, and headed north up to the homeless shelter.

Ricky came back one more time for lunch, but after that we never saw him again.

***

Were we merciful to Ricky?

I thought about that after we discharged him.

Of course, I was a drinker, but I knew enough not to drink at Graced Opportunities. In any case, I didn't have to. I could tag along with my college friends at their business dinners and pound drafts of Guinness stout while they talked about "what the market wants." I could crash with Liz, my ex- and future girlfriend who lived in Hoboken—and in the mornings go to an Italian deli by her apartment and feast on cannoli and biscotti to soak up the alcohol from the night before.

But Ricky—he had no other place to go.

I could admit that it wasn't fair.

But those were the rules we all had to abide by. I always suspected that Sister Virginia had been too merciful—maybe it was that second chance she gave to a resident that got her killed. I didn't know for sure, but I did know that we couldn't handle heroin, cocaine, and box cutters. That was the truth of the situation—mercy was just wishful thinking.

Were we merciful to Ricky?

I think about it a little differently now.

"Mercy and truth are met together," according to Psalm 85:10 (KJV). The academic in me is uncomfortable taking it out of context, but it was a line repeated to me by a friend when we were talking about our continuing recovery from alcoholism. Confronting people with the truth about themselves is harsh and dreadful—but it can be an act of love. It can also be experienced as mercy, if and when people finally accept the truth about themselves.

Ricky couldn't accept the truth about himself at that time— nor could I have accepted the truth about myself if someone had confronted me about my drinking.

But mercy and truth often do meet—even though we may fight against such a meeting with all the weapons we have at our disposal.

Mercy and truth met for me on the South Side of Chicago.

I hope they eventually met for Ricky.

Maybe Sister Virginia wasn't being too merciful—if being merciful is understood as being sentimental or foolhardy. Maybe she reached out to that resident in both mercy and truth—and he responded violently, killing the messenger to eliminate the message.

I never knew Sister Virginia.

But maybe she didn't lose her life as much as she gave it—gave it in witness to how mercy and truth come together in a harsh and dreadful love.

Suggested Questions for Discussion

1. In what ways do truth and honesty figure into these stories in the chapter?
2. What do you think about how Graced Opportunities approached the homeless problem? Was it merciful?
3. How would you have dealt with Ricky?
4. Is revealing the truth always merciful?

Suggested Questions for Private Reflection

1. When confronted with a truth about yourself, how do you react?
2. Has there been a time when someone said something harsh to you that you were able later to experience as merciful?

PART THREE

MERCY AND GOD

Chapter Nine

Mercy and Forgiveness

*Because of the strength and hope of the victims, the story of the
Boston Marathon bombing became something more than an
account of a horrible crime and its terrible aftermath.*

It was four days after the Boston Marathon bombing, April 19,
2013.[1] I was in a van driving to the airport through a deserted
Boston. The whole city was locked down—the bombers had yet
to be caught. Security at Logan International Airport was tight
with armed guards and vehicle inspections.

In terminal C—the terminal where the 9/11 hijackers board-
ed their planes to New York City—I joined other travelers around
a television and we nervously watched news feeds about the search
for suspects.

There was a palpable sense of fear and anger.

Over the next couple of days, the bombing's terrible toll began
to be tallied. We learned the names of the dead: Krystle Campbell, twenty-nine years old, from Medford; Lu Lingzi, twenty-
three years old, a graduate student at Boston University; Martin
Richard, eight years old, who liked soccer, basketball, and baseball. Sean Collier, a police office at the Massachusetts Institute of
Technology, also was murdered—shot and killed three days after the bombing. The bombs were pressure cookers, armed with
blasting caps, hidden in backpacks among the crowd. Altogether,
more than 260 people were injured, including seventeen people
who lost limbs. By the end of the manhunt, one of the perpetra-

tors, Tamerlan Tsarnaev was dead. His brother and accomplice, Dzhokhar Tsarnaev, was in custody.

***

By the Monday after the attacks, I had returned from my trip and was in my office preparing for classes.

There was a knock on my door and it was Rachel. I invited her in, and she sat in a futon chair across from me and next to the five-foot white teddy bear I have in the office as my personal mascot. I sat in a wingback chair facing her—I never talk to students over my desk. It's so messy that I wouldn't be able to see them.

It created a rather surreal setting given the subject under discussion.

"We're going to talk about the Boston Marathon bombing, right?" Rachel asked. Rachel was in Holy Cross' College Honors Program, which I was directing at the time, and she was a student in the special honors seminar I was teaching: *Religion and Violence.*

"I'm not sure we can handle it," I said. It probably would have been more honest to say, "I'm not sure I can handle it as a teacher."

Even under normal circumstances, the *Religion and Violence* seminar was not a typical class. We had talked about the Aztecs and Al-Qaeda, the Crusades and jihad, the Provisional IRA and Al-Aqsa Martyrs brigade. Along the way we had intense debates about the ethics of collateral damage during warfare, suicide bombings, and the use of weapons of mass destruction.

Those questions involved other places and other people, separated from us by seemingly vast distances of time and space.

Not anymore.

Rachel wouldn't put up with my hesitation and doubts: "We can handle it—it's what college is about. We need to talk about the issues so many of us are struggling with." She was insistent.

And she was right.

The seminar convened the next day, Tuesday. Up until that point in the seminar, I had been an aggressive instructor, relentlessly challenging student statements and assumptions. This time, I wanted to have students share their views and experiences freely—so I tried to facilitate gently and not to press or confront.

And students shared. Sarah, whose mother was running the marathon, talked about how connected she felt to others, especially through #bostonstrong Twitter messages. Annette, a classics major, shared how everyone on her hall watched the hunt for Tamerlan and Dzhokhar Tsarnaev on television and how everyone cheered when they were caught. There was a sense of community, a feeling of solidarity, Annette remembered.

Soon difficult questions began to emerge.

Rachel stepped up and mentioned that we had learned about how violence begets violence. She asked, "Does our urge to condemn, and lash out, bring a temptation to be violent ourselves in a way that creates more victims?" Samuel agreed with this point and argued that given the "bitter anger that arises from such an event, we tend to eventually generalize that hate to entire groups of people." Many students feared that their Muslim friends and classmates might be caught in the backlash.

The discussion then turned to forgiveness and whether we should forgive the perpetrators. Connor raised the type of question I would have asked if it had been a normal class: "Does our talk about forgiveness run the risk of making a moral decision that should be left to the injured, and the families and friends of those who were killed?"

All Christians know Jesus' words: "Do not resist one who is evil. But if any one strikes you on the right cheek, turn to him the other also" (Mt 5:39). Taken literally, this is one of the most challenging of Jesus' teachings. Paradoxically, perhaps, that admonition is easier to accept if you're simply talking about yourself: someone might decide to forgive a crime that affected them personally, but that's different from telling someone else that they must do the same.

But Rachel and Connor were talking not just about mercy and violence in connection to the Christian obligation to forgive, but also about the social ramifications of being merciful to those who commit violence. Mercy to the killers might be a way of responding to violence by breaking the cycle of recrimination and revenge. But that very same mercy also ran the risk of another kind of violence by insulting the many victims and the memory of those who were killed.

***

One of the most difficult tenets of Christianity for Christians of all stripes to fully embrace is the concept of forgiveness. Why should anyone who deliberately commits a heinous act against me personally, a relative or friend, or society at large, be forgiven?

We've all heard the remarkable stories of victims forgiving their assailants: the father of a young woman murdered by the Green River Killer; the young New York City police officer shot and paralyzed by a teenager; the man shot three times by the Aurora, Colorado, theater gunman.

Catholicism values praying for criminals, such as St. Thérèse of Lisieux did when she asked God for the repentance of the murderer Henri Pranzini before he faced the guillotine.

Catholicism also celebrates seemingly incomprehensible acts of forgiveness, such as St. Maria Goretti's willingness to pardon Alessandro Serenelli, the man who mortally wounded her. After the assassination attempt that nearly claimed his life, St. John Paul II met with Mehmet Ali Agca and spoke to him as a brother. Agca was eventually released, served jail time in Turkey, and went to Rome to place flowers on the tomb of the man he once tried to kill. In this sense, forgiveness speaks to the deepest Christian belief that no one lies beyond the mercy of God.

If that is so, what does it mean for our understanding of Tamerlan and Dzhokhar Tsarnaev?

***

News reports after the bombing tried to define Tamerlan Tsarnaev: he was a son, brother, husband, father, American, Chechen,
Muslim, boxer, killer, terrorist. But no one could really put all of
those together in a neat package that would explain why he did
what he did.

And when Tamerlan's body came to a Worcester funeral
home—only a short drive from the Holy Cross campus—we had a
stranger in our midst, and no one knew quite what to do with him.

Protests grew on the sidewalk outside the funeral home.
Nerves were raw throughout Central Massachusetts: the Boston
Marathon bombing was not simply a local tragedy; it was a crime
committed against our families, our neighbors, our friends.

National media coverage focused on the criticism of the funeral home's owner when he agreed to take the body when it was
clear that no one else wanted to. But local news reporting was far
more nuanced, surveying the range of ways all of us in Worcester
were working through our feelings about the bombing and its
perpetrators, all the while trying to find hope within and through
our anger and sense of loss. The issue drew perceptive and wry
commentary, such as that by columnist Diane Williamson who
suggested that the body be taken by the developers pushing for a
controversial slot-machine initiative.[2]

"I do understand no one wants to associate their names with
such evil events."[3] So said Ruslan Tsarni, who came to Worcester
to perform the burial rites for his nephew. Death has always raised
the specter of contagion. It's one reason why we have cemeteries.
For some, putting Tamerlan Tsarnaev in the ground was allowing
him a permanent place among us—a presence too close to those
who had been wounded so deeply. Denying him burial became
the only way to decisively condemn him and his acts. For its part,
Cambridge would not allow Tamerlan to be buried within city
limits. His body lay in a North Attleborough funeral home until
it came to Worcester.

"We are burying a dead body. That's what we do."[4] So said Worcester funeral director Peter Stefan. Society entrusts some people with the tasks the rest of us don't want to do. One of those is burying the dead, and someone has to do it. One can interpret this as a simple bureaucratic fact, but it attests to something deeper. "I cannot separate the sin from the sinner," Stefan explained.[5] And he was right—none of us could. Which is why everyone seemed paralyzed, not knowing what mercy really meant in such a complicated situation.

But then Worcester Police announced that a "courageous and compassionate individual" had come forward to transport the remains out of Worcester.[6] Soon, it was revealed that the remains were accepted by an "interfaith coalition" in Doswell, Virginia, and Tamerlan Tsarnaev was interned in an unmarked grave in a local Muslim cemetery.[7]

Putting Tamerlan in the ground certainly did not bring closure to his many victims. But we all do return to the ground inevitably. Burying Tamerlan Tsarnaev was paradoxically an act of faith and hope, affirming that a connection exists between us all, even though that connection may itself be buried, and hidden from our sight.

"Jesus tells us, 'Love your enemies.' Not to hate them, even after they are dead."[8] So said Martha Mullen, who coordinated efforts to arrange for the transport and burial of Tamerlan Tsarnaev—the stranger in our midst.

The Muslim and Christian members of the interfaith coalition in Doswell were strangers to many of us in Worcester.

They brought us mercy by taking on a burden none of us could bear alone.

***

Dzhokhar Tsarnaev came to trial on January 5, 2015, nearly two years after the bombing and the burial of his brother.

As the trial commenced, most of the discussion surrounded not whether Dzhokhar Tsarnaev was guilty, but whether he should be given the death penalty.

Governor-elect Charlie Baker suggested that Dzhokhar Tsarnaev was a criminal worthy only of being despised—someone who deserved a punishment that matches the severity of the crime for which he was accused.[9] The Catholic bishops of Massachusetts had a more nuanced position, and reiterated Pope Francis' conclusion that the death penalty "is an offense against the inviolability of life and the dignity of the human person."[10] The bishops made clear that Catholic teaching does not forbid capital punishment totally, but in cases like that of Dzhokhar Tsarnaev, the "ability to cause harm is not current, as it has been neutralized."[11] Accordingly, since the person "is already deprived of their liberty," then "no matter how heinous the crime, if society can protect itself without ending a human life, it should do so."[12]

A Catholic perspective on sin and forgiveness would emphasize necessity of both contrition and penance. Contrition means that the sinner feels genuine remorse for the sin committed; penance reflects a desire to atone, to make restitution so that the demands of justice are satisfied. So, forgiving someone for a heinous act does not mean they should go unpunished.

But for many, the real issue was that Dzhokhar Tsarnaev had shown no remorse for his actions. While many took that fact as an argument against mercy of any kind, it could also be taken to emphasize that mercy is needed even more strongly. Mercy can bring a new awareness and a new life to those who need it most— that is, the perpetrators of violence who, as Christ said, "know not what they do" (Lk 23: 34).

Dzhokhar Tsarnaev finally did ask for mercy—during the penalty phase of the trial, after he had been found guilty. In a prepared statement he began, in the name of Allah, "the exalted and glorious, the most gracious, the most merciful."[13] He apologized, saying: "Now, I am sorry for the lives that I've taken, for the suffering that I've caused you, for the damage that I've done. Irreparable damage."[14] He then asked for mercy: "I ask Allah to have mercy upon me and my brother and my family. I ask Allah to bestow his mercy upon those present here today."[15]

Some of the victims and families of the dead were not persuaded by Dzhokhar Tsarnaev's statement of apology, carefully crafted as it clearly was. Lynn Julien was quoted as saying, "There was nothing simple about what he said and there was nothing sincere."[16] But Henry Borgard, another survivor, said: "For me to hear him say he is sorry, that is enough for me. And I hope because I still do have faith in humanity, including in him, I hope that his words were genuine. I hope they were heartfelt."[17]

For me, what was significant was that Dzhokhar Tsarnaev did not mention any of the victims, particularly the dead, by name. Moreover, while he did seem to recognize the magnitude of the pain and suffering he had caused and took responsibility as a perpetrator, He did not seem to renounce violence or the justifications for it that he and his brother seemed to espouse. He did not go as far as to say that his actions had been wrong or misguided at the outset.

But mercy recognizes that God's perspective and time frame are not ours. In God's eyes, the circle closes with the repentance of the sinner. Mercy provides a space and opportunity for repentance in a way not allowed by an uncompromising sentence of death. The problem for us is that we do not have God's vantage point—or God's patience.

Dzhokhar Tsarnaev was sentenced to death. He is now imprisoned at the ADX maximum security prison in Florence, Colorado.[18] Barring a pardon or successful appeal, he will eventually be executed at the federal prison in Terre Haute, Indiana.

***

As the Dzhokhar Tsarnaev trial was beginning, I contacted the students in the *Religion and Violence* seminar again. They were now seniors and I wanted not only to check my facts about the class discussion two years earlier, but also wanted to ask them their thoughts now that Tsarnaev was finally coming to trial. All seemed to emphasize that forgiveness was the most appropriate response in the wake of the attack. Ellen, an English major, reflected that as heinous as the crime was, hatred would never satisfy us. Rachel spoke for many students when she wrote to me, "Forgiving does not mean forgetting—instead, it requires remembrance, remembrance of what was done, and remembrance of the victims."

During the penalty phase of the trial, victims of the bombing gave impact statements. Among the most moving was the testimony from Bill Richard, whose eight-year-old son, Martin, was killed. Referring to Dzhokhar Tsarnaev's refusal to stop his brother Tamerlan, Richard said: "He chose to do nothing. He chose destruction. He chose death."[19] But then, Richard added, "We choose love. We choose kindness. We choose peace. This is our response to hate."[20] Jennifer Kauffman, who had suffered post-traumatic stress and ear injuries after the bombing, said to Dzhokhar Tsarnaev: "I forgive you and your brother. My hope and desire is someday soon you'll be brave enough to take responsibility for your actions and forgo all your appeals, so we can all move together in peace."[21]

Forgiveness is a not sign of weakness, but of strength; forgiveness is not resignation, it is hope. Because of the strength and hope of the victims, the story of the Boston Marathon bombing became something more than an account of a horrible crime and its terrible aftermath. Though forgiveness does lie finally in the hands of God, the mercy of forgiveness can aid the work of healing. While Dzhokhar Tsarnaev does need to deepen his repentance, he also needs healing—and it does not diminish the seriousness of his crime to pray that he might reconcile with the victims, with God, and find forgiveness. In praying that he might be forgiven, we also pray for the victims and their families that they might find mercy as well.

Opening ourselves up to the possibility of mercy and forgiveness for someone else is often a hard journey. What makes it especially hard is confronting how mercy and forgiveness for someone else is intertwined with our own need for hope and healing.

Suggested Questions for Discussion

1. What do you think of the issues that the students raised about the Boston Marathon bombing? What issues occur to you?
2. Should Tamerlan Tsarnaev have been given burial on U.S. soil?
3. Was Dzhokhar Tsarnaev's apology sufficient?
4. Should we show Dzhokhar Tsarnaev mercy? What would that mean?

Suggested Questions for Private Reflection

1. Do you believe in forgiveness for yourself and others?
2. What can you forgive? What do you have trouble forgiving?

Chapter Ten

Mercy and Suffering

*In the killing fields of Sri Lanka—not all of which have been
uncovered—the road to mercy cannot come at the price
of ignoring God's admonitions not to murder as well as
not to bear false witness. Mercy must include
both justice and truth.*

It certainly wasn't happenstance that Pope Francis chose Divine
Mercy Sunday for the proclamation of the extraordinary Jubilee
of Mercy.[1] It was a choice that marked a point of continuity between his pontificate and those of his predecessors. Popes Benedict XVI and St. John Paul II were both instrumental in spreading
devotion to the Divine Mercy throughout the world.

But it's also important to remember that emphasizing God's
mercy does have a long history within the Catholic Christian tra-
dition. Medieval artists depicted God's "throne of Mercy" and the
image of "God's throne of Grace" goes back to St. Paul's Letter to
the Hebrews.

But if the mercy of God is one of the most prominent themes
in Christian understandings of God, it's also the most problem-
atic. Simply put, how can a merciful God allow so much human
suffering?

***

On Good Friday 2014, I lingered after a beautiful service at the
College of the Holy Cross. I sat in the back row and fixed my eyes
on a large wooden cross behind the altar. The cross was tied with
rough-twined rope at the place where the horizontal and vertical
beams met.

I tried to simply repeat the name of Jesus—silently, reverently, so that it would merge with the rhythm of my breathing.

I wanted to quiet my mind.

But my mind wandered.

I thought about friends who had died too soon. I thought of loved ones struggling with intractable illnesses. I remembered brilliant teachers and gifted students who felt themselves unnoticed and unloved.

Where was God's mercy for them?

More thoughts came to me—thoughts of the self-pitying, self-indulgent kind, thoughts of times when I suffered and wondered where God's mercy was for me.

***

I forced my mind farther afield, to an experience I had the previous year.

It was 2013 and I was traveling in a car with a friend in Sri Lanka.

I could tell when we had left the Sinhalese Buddhist heartland and were entering into the predominantly Tamil northern part of the island: police stations and military barracks were stationed behind berms, with dug-in sentry points, and fortified by barbed wire and gates marked by gilded regimental crests. The rural Tamil areas were marked not as towns, but as sectors. Though there were clear-cuts spots to help with de-mining operations, the area was still lush and green, dotted by small reservoirs and rice paddies.

We first visited the shrine to Our Lady of Madhu, Sri Lanka's largest Catholic pilgrimage site, where Pope Francis would say Mass a year later.[2] We then decided to take a short cut to another shrine, this one to the Passion of the Christ, and found ourselves driving along a dirt road in the jungle.

Nailed to the coconut palms lining the road were signs with diagrams and photos explaining how to identify claymore mines, improvised explosive devices, undetonated shells and grenades—a warning for travelers about the leftovers of war still lurking in the thick foliage. We exited the car only once—and very carefully—to investigate a snake on the roadside.

We emerged from the jungle into a village that was still in the process of rebuilding. The walls of some of the homes were gouged and pitted from the fighting; other homes were clearly improvised from whatever was available, such as thatch, wood, and corrugated tin.

***

The Sri Lankan civil war began as an insurrection among the minority Tamil-speaking community to establish a separate state, called "Eelam," that would allow freedom from the country's Sinhalese-speaking majority. In 1983, the insurgent group known as the Liberation Tigers of Tamil Eelam ambushed a military convoy and killed fourteen soldiers. In response, many in the Singhalese majority rioted and launched a pogrom that killed thousands of Tamils during a period that Tamils now call "Black July."

It was the Sri Lankan civil war that saw the first large-scale use of suicide bombings, which the Liberation Tigers of Tamil Eelam used not only to terrorize military personnel and civilians, but also for assassination attacks that killed Sri Lankan President Ranasinghe Premadasa and former Indian Prime Minister Rajiv Gandhi. The Liberation Tigers of Tamil Eelam carved out enough territory for themselves in the northern part of the island to maintain their own state for nearly two decades until their final defeat by the Sri Lankan army in 2009.

The Tamil and Singhalese speaking populations are both members of Sri Lanka's significant Catholic minority that traces its origins to the work of St. Joseph Vaz, a seventeenth-century Oratorian priest from Portugal's Indian colony of Goa. The civil war exposed deep fractures in Sri Lanka Catholicism, and Catholics could be found one both sides during the conflict. For example, the lead spokesman for the Liberation Tigers of Tamil

Eelam was the diocesan vicar and head of the Catholic seminary in the Tamil-speaking city of Jaffna. But Catholics also served in leadership positions in the Sri Lankan army.

For its part, the Catholic Church could never develop a coherent response to the conflict. One time, Tamil-speaking Catholic bishops proposed a Christmas cease-fire only to be rebuffed by their brother bishops who had dioceses in Singhalese speaking areas.

***

We found the Shrine to the Passion of the Christ in the war-torn village. Billboards in Madhu, and along the dirt road in the jungle, portrayed the shrine as an important pilgrimage site. But when we entered, it was close to empty—there were only a few field laborers sitting on the floor, nonchalantly enjoying a lunch of rice and curry.

The church was as dilapidated as the surrounding buildings. I thought: here it is, the heart of desolation, destruction, abandonment.

Once again, that subversive thought surfaced: Where was God's mercy?

The center of the shrine was a large statue of Christ scourged. He wore a crown of thorns and a red cloak. The lashes on His body were painted bright red, with drops of blood detailed on His chest, arms, and face. His eyes looked up and His lips were parted as if He was about to speak.

Here is the God who suffers—suffers for us, suffers with us.

***

For Pope Francis, the suffering God is the merciful God. God enters into our own experiences of suffering to provide comfort and consolation in unexpected ways. Of course, Pope Francis has said a lot about mercy and many books have been published that bring together his diverse and varied reflections. Usually, Pope Francis' penetrating insights come in the form of concise commentaries, aphorisms, and the occasional off-the-cuff sound bite.

A more academically sustained discussion of mercy can be found in the writings of Cardinal Walter Kasper, formerly the president of the Pontifical Council for Promoting Christian Unity. Cardinal Kasper and Pope Francis are reported to be quite close, and Cardinal Kasper has been described as "The Pope's Theologian."

During the pontificate of Pope Benedict XVI, Cardinal Kasper published *Mercy: The Essence of the Gospel and Key to the Christian Life*.[3] The central theme of the book is developing a coherent understanding of Christian mercy. Cardinal Kasper realizes all too well that one of the greatest criticisms that atheists make against Christianity is that it is simply incoherent to believe in a merciful God who is all-powerful, a loving Creator, who nonetheless allows human suffering.

Cardinal Kasper reflects on mercy through the ancient Latin term "*misericordia*," which he defines as having a "'heart' with the poor."[4] Taken in this sense, mercy doesn't eliminate suffering. Humans suffer: that much we know in our fallen world. Rather, in Cardinal Kasper's view, mercy responds to suffering, whether it's the suffering that comes from poverty or persecution or the suffering coming from a simple lack of love.

Mercy is a connection, not a cure from above.

Cardinal Kasper argues that mercy is the essence of God— the quality from which all others proceed. In making this statement, the cardinal has been criticized for lack of theological and philosophical rigor. For example, in a look at Cardinal Kasper's views on mercy, Father Daniel P. Moloney argues that since mercy responds to sin or some other imperfection, mercy cannot be part of God's essence because God does not show mercy to himself.[5] Father Moloney maintains that it would be better to say that God's mercy proceeds from His love—and that love is truly part of the essence of God in a way that mercy is not.[6]

But Cardinal Kasper wants us to know that God suffers with us. He argues that God's suffering with us isn't a sign of weakness; rather, it is sign of God's strength, God's choice to surrender to love.[7]

We must make the same choice.

Cardinal Kasper argues that Christians are required to promote a culture of mercy. He reflects at length on the challenges of globalization and the gap between the rich countries of the North and the poor countries of the South. But he does not want Christianity to become a political program—that would be "Christian totalitarianism."[8] Instead, mercy forces us to ask in concrete terms: What do human beings need in order to be human beings with full freedom and dignity?

***

Seeing my Sri Lanka experience in my mind's eye during prayer on Good Friday wasn't something random, but it also wasn't some sort of mystical insight or illumination.

I had been thinking about—no, struggling with—that Sri Lanka experience intently as I thought about Pope Francis' call for a Jubilee of Mercy.

I decided to read Cardinal Kasper's book as part of that effort.

Applying his more philosophical reflections on mercy would be a challenging task in Sri Lanka.

Though the civil war ended seven years ago, thousands of Sri Lankans remain unaccounted for. There were human-rights violations and war crimes on both sides—massacres, rapes, and torture. Tens of thousands of Sri Lankans died and hundreds of thousands were displaced. Hundreds more have been killed by the war's leftovers—land mines, injuries, disease.

Surely it was merciful that the conflict ended, but where was God's mercy when it began? We can speak of mercy for those wounded and displaced. But what about mercy for the killers who remain alive? What about justice for the dead?

Cardinal Kasper warns us against what he calls "pseudo-mercy." Pseudo-mercy is not just misplaced indulgence or a lack of courage that cannot bear to tell the truth—though pseudo-mercy can involve such sins of omission. Instead, pseudo-mercy implicitly ridicules God's commandments. For example, Cardinal Kasper talks about how assisted suicide is pseudo-mercy that violates the commandment "Thou shalt not murder."[9]

In the killing fields of Sri Lanka—not all of which have been uncovered—the road to mercy cannot come at the price of ignoring God's admonitions not to murder as well as not to bear false witness. Mercy must include both justice and truth, which is why the United Nations has consistently maintained that allegations of war crimes during the Sri Lankan civil war must be fully investigated.

While Cardinal Kasper's argument might have some interesting implications for global politics both in South Asia and beyond, for an academic like me, the aspect I most appreciated about his discussion was how it engaged contemporary critics of religion I had read in graduate school. I have to admit that being in a former war zone definitely put the academic life in perspective—its "ivy-covered towers" seem privileged and distant when the people around you are collecting brush and leaves to roof their homes.

At the shrine, I suppose, I could have talked to the people having lunch and asked what they thought about the image of the scourged Christ with His eyes raised to heaven and His mouth parted.

I could have asked: What do you hear Christ saying?

I could have asked: Does God suffer? Is God all-powerful? What is mercy?

But would my questions even have made sense in that context? Maybe Cardinal Kasper's book—so filled with systematic theological reflections—would have been not just untranslatable but also strangely irrelevant.

***

The suffering Christ was not the only image in the shrine that day in Sri Lanka. Off to the side was a poster of the glorified Christ, in a white gown, His pierced right hand raised in blessing. Christ's left hand pointed to His heart, and from His heart emanated two rays of light: one red and one pale white/blue.

This was a reproduction of the Divine Mercy, originally painted at the direction of Sister Faustina Kowalska—a Polish nun, visionary, and stigmatist who died in 1938. As she had recorded in her spiritual diary, Christ had asked that the Sunday after Easter be specially consecrated to Divine Mercy.[10]

For a time, the Vatican prohibited dissemination of images and writings associated with Sister Faustina and the Divine Mercy devotion. One concern was that there was perhaps too much focus on Sister Faustina herself, as well as potential theological difficulties with some claims she made about the remission of sins outside of the Sacrament of Penance. It was only under the pontificate of St. John Paul II that her reputation was fully rehabilitated. In fact, St. John Paul proclaimed Sister Faustina the first saint of the new millennium.

Seeing the Divine Mercy in Sri Lanka wasn't that surprising, since the devotion has become popular the world over. But as popular as it is, both the devotion and St. Faustina herself still have their critics. Some are concerned that the more ancient traditions associated with the Second Sunday of Easter have been displaced in favor of a contemporary devotion of dubious origins. Some simply do not see St. Faustina's visions as genuine.

Given these suspicions about St. Faustina and the Divine Mercy devotion, it did come as a surprise to me when Cardinal Kasper referenced her prayer in his quite scholarly reflections on mercy. St. Faustina's prayer begins, "Help me, O Lord, that my eyes may be merciful so that I may never suspect or judge from appearances, but look for what is beautiful in my neighbors' souls and come to their rescue."[11]

Mercy involves concrete acts: forgiveness, consolation, patience, and solidarity.

But mercy begins and ends with a prayerful union with the Crucified and Resurrected Christ that allows us to see our neighbor in a new way.

***

I didn't stay long in the Shrine to the Passion of the Christ in Sri Lanka—I took my pictures and departed since it was going to be a long drive back.

I also didn't stay that long after the Good Friday service at the college chapel. I tried to look at the cross for as long as possible. I reflected on my Sri Lanka experience as much as I could, but realized that I wasn't going to be able to make complete sense of God's mercy in that context—or any other.

The Holy Year is an extended opportunity not only for us to reflect on God's mercy in our own lives, but also to bring mercy into the lives of others. There will also be opportunities for discussions of the more academic kind, such as how Pope Francis is explicitly and implicitly drawing upon a range of theologians and mystics when he speaks of the mercy of God and reminds us that "God never tires of forgiving us."[12]

It is surely the case that many of us never tire of being forgiven. But the demanding, difficult questions surrounding God's mercy and the grinding reality of suffering are personally and collectively tiring. They frequently exhaust our abilities to comprehend or understand. The pain and tension seem never-ending.

In her diary, St. Faustina often writes of the "abyss" of misery.[13] But she also describes God's mercy as an "abyss."[14]

During this extraordinary Jubilee of Mercy, Pope Francis seems to be asking us to follow St. Faustina's example and enter into an abyss of both misery and mercy—to "have our hearts" in and with both, and to linger longer than seems comfortable.

It is then, perhaps, that we can fully experience what is often so hard to understand: God's love is present to each and every one of us.

Suggested Questions for Discussion

1. If you were at the shrine in Sri Lanka, what questions would you have asked?
2. What does it mean to experience mercy in the context of suffering? Think about a specific example, either in your own life or the life of someone you know.
3. Is mercy supposed to cure suffering or is the connection more complex?
4. When you think about God's mercy, what image comes to mind?

Suggested Questions for Private Reflection

1. Have you ever had an experience that challenged your sense of a merciful God? If so, how did you respond?
2. How might you respond to someone who questions God's mercy?

Chapter Eleven

Mercy and Death

"You know, Mathew, I've been thinking a lot about Jesus."
I nod, indicating that I want to hear more. "What Jesus did—
it was all really simple: it was all about love."

"Jesus, please let Dad have a merciful death."

Incense, diesel exhaust, and the smell of fresh flowers hung in the air. It was noisy, too—two stoke engines buzzed, storekeepers hawked their wares, people talked loudly in languages I didn't know. I saw multicolored lights flashing around a large sign: "The more you honour me, the more I will bless you."

It was January 2013 and sunny and warm outside, and here I was escaping a conference at Bangalore's Christ University where I had just presented on the legacy of Vatican II.

Please, Jesus, a merciful death. "The more you honour me, the more I will bless you."

At the Infant Jesus Shrine, I couldn't let it go: What about the theology implied by the sign? Does Jesus demand honor as a precondition for His mercy?

I didn't think that I could actually change Jesus by honoring Him—but I did think that the process of honoring Jesus could change me, and help me find a way through my feelings of helplessness in the face my father's impending death.

The Shrine to the Infant Jesus is a compound open to the street—there's a church, the shrine itself, and a grotto. First, I went to the grotto and lit a candle: "Hail Mary, full of grace . . ." "Our Father, who art in heaven . . ." and placed a hundred-rupee note (about

$1.50) in the collection box. I then went to the main shrine. A large Infant of Prague statue, dressed in white silk and lace and topped by a golden crown, was elevated on an altar and set under a canopy supported by four pillars and ringed by lights—the kind of lights that you'd see hanging on Christmas trees in the United States.[1] There were two other Infant of Prague statues, dressed in purple silk with gold and red crowns, standing on pedestals rising from the chapel floor. I purchased a large flour garland and adorned one of the statues. I then gently placed my right hand on the statue's right foot and said a prayer for my father.

In praying for a merciful death for my father, I meant a death without physical pain and suffering. Pain and suffering had been foremost on my mind because my father had been diagnosed with inoperable lung cancer.

Dad did die a merciful death just a month later. But since his passing, I have come to realize that my initial understanding of mercy and death was much too narrow in its exclusive focus on physical pain and suffering. Opening oneself to mercy at death, as my father did, and asking God for mercy for all of us as a family, as I did, is about something more fundamental than avoiding pain and suffering.

***

A couple of weeks before I prayed at the Infant Jesus Shrine, I was with my mother and father in a hospital room in Maine. Mom and Dad were sitting side by side on the hospital bed, hand-in-hand. Someone had placed a chair at the foot of the bed, opposite the door, and there I waited. The doctor was due any minute. My father had been told earlier that morning that his lung cancer could not be cured, but I still needed convincing because I thought it was so unfair. I couldn't get over the shock of it all. Dad had quit smoking over twenty years before and only six months earlier had had a chest X-ray that showed no abnormalities.

The doctor arrived.

We greeted him and asked for an elaboration of the diagnosis. He grabbed a green marker that was stuck to a Velcro pad right next to the whiteboard where nurses would record their visits and list the medications they administered. He drew a diagram of my father's lungs and made a dot to indicate the tumor. He circled the dot and drew lines coming from it, crossing the boundaries of the lungs.

He talked to the whiteboard, "By definition, the cancer is inoperable because it has spread beyond the chest."

The doctor made a couple of more diagnostic statements facing the board and finally turned around to face my parents.

"Yes, doctor, we understand, thank you so much," Dad said, and Mom put her arm around him.

I bowed my head as my parents embraced.

Dad was eighty-six years old. He had lived a long and full life. He wasn't a diagram.

Still, I wonder what was appropriate to expect in that context. Humans are both body and soul—my Catholic training taught me that. It was the doctor's responsibility to treat my father's symptoms: his body. The doctor probably hadn't received very much training in talking through the emotional and spiritual aspects of death and dying—the "soul" part. There was a social worker at the hospital who handled that, offering referrals to those who were religious. Dad was in the spiritual-but-not-religious category and, in any case, my mom was there for him—and that was all the spiritual support he needed at that moment. But I still felt as though the whole process could have been less disjointed—and more merciful.

***

Dad had a beard and thinning white hair. His nose and ears seemed large because he was short, about five feet four inches.

He was small, and he liked small things.

Dad had a collection of miniatures. His prized possessions were silver pillboxes set with delicate inlay and precious stones.

He appreciated delicacy in more mundane things, too. The best present Caroline and I ever gave him was a small, single-egg frying pan.

He thought it was big enough to cook food for two.

While often symbolized by small things, like the exchange of rings, marriage is obviously no small thing. My mother and father had been married over sixty years, and they went by the collective title "Dick and Do," Mom's name being pronounced "dough." Mom definitely knew how to respond—calmly and lovingly—to exclamations like: "Do, there's a problem with the washing machine. Don't touch it, get out the instruction manual, and get on the phone to India, China, or wherever!"

Sometimes, the small things got my dad flustered, too.

Mom and Dad—"Dick and Do"—taught my sister, Julia, and me that marriage is built on many small acts of love: a gentle handhold, flowers carefully arranged by the bedside, sometimes even brief and gentle scoldings followed by a tender embrace. Dad had a special phrase that he used to describe their marriage. He'd say, "I cast my bread out on the waters and it comes back Do."

Whenever he'd repeat those words, he'd comment, "It's epigrammatic, you know," then slyly look around to see whether anyone understood that he meant not "Do, Re, Me," but how his bread was actually Do.

***

Dad was a college art history professor by profession. He was comfortable with the lecture style and would often take the smallest topic and expand on it in grandiose ways—setting the clocks back for daylight savings would bring reflections on time and consciousness; a strange noise coming from the computer would bring denunciations of technology as a threat to human dignity.

But Dad was also an artist, a watercolorist. His paintings were sophisticated renderings of light and color: the sun's play on a gray New England farmhouse as snow fell; the shadings of twilight amid the green and browns of an oak-covered hill. As much as I tried, I could never see colors as my father saw them. He saw cerulean or cobalt—I only saw blue.

One time, when I was very little, I asked about what it was like to paint, and Dad said, "Painting is like praying."

It was only during the last decade of his life, when he started to paint still lifes, that I began to understand what he meant. The alternatively vibrant and subtle colors, the delicate intertwining of the shapes and forms, gave witness to the great and expansive beauty that lies before us, if we would only pause long enough to notice.

My father's paintings *were* prayers: they were visions of a transfigured world—the world as created and transformed by the merciful love of God.

When we believe in that merciful love, we see beauty in the small things, everywhere, all the time.

***

"You know, Mathew," Dad said sitting in the chair in his apartment. I was just back from India. "I'm going to go through all of the stages: denial, anger, bargaining, depression, and, hopefully, acceptance." His breathing was getting labored; the cancer was advancing; he was in between trips to the hospital. He was wearing big fleece slippers and was dressed in warm-up pants and a sweatshirt. He would often recycle sweatshirts that I wore in my college days—a blue Bruce Springsteen sweatshirt was his favorite. But that day, he was wearing one of his own—a gray sweatshirt he got after going on a cruise to Antarctica with his younger brother, Bob.

He said, "Part of me will rejoin nature—that's why I've chosen to be cremated. Everything goes in cycles. We come from the earth and go back to her."

Dad converted to Catholicism back in the 1950s. He came from a well-to-do Boston family that was not very religious and certainly not enthused about the smells and bells of Catholicism along with its seemingly rigid hierarchical structure. When I became a professor myself, Dad gave me the books he read in those days. A family friend had given him Paul Blanshard's *American Freedom and Catholic Power*, a screed arguing that being Catholic and being American were fundamentally incompatible.[2] But along with the anti-Catholic tracts, there were books that supported his conversion, writings by Thomas Merton and, most precious to him, works from the Jesuit theologian and scientist Teilhard de Chardin. Teilhard's thought prefigured much of today's environmental theology—including Pope Francis' encyclical *Laudato Si'*.[3] Teilhard's most fundamental point was that the complexity of nature allows us to appreciate how God creates all things and draws everything to himself.

I heard echoes of Teilhard as my father was speaking about his death.

"What can I do to help as things progress?" I asked. I still couldn't say what I really meant: How can I help you feel mercy as you prepare to die?

Dad wasn't the one experiencing denial—I was.

"We'll just take things as they come," Dad said. "Mom and I have already planned things out."

Logistically, there wasn't very much for me to do. In any case, my sister, Julia, who was preparing to fly in from Virginia, was on top of making plans for assisted living should that become necessary.

But I wasn't ready to let go. I thought about my upcoming spring break and looked forward to being able to spend that time with Dad. I hoped we could renew the religious discussions we'd had when I was younger, when we'd talk about subjects such as St. Anselm's teleological proof of God's existence or St. Thomas Aquinas' views on grace. As death approached, I wondered what Dad would say about some of the theological issues that we once probed together.

Maybe talking with him would allow me to see death—and life—in a new way.

Religious discussions between my father and me had become rarer since he had stopped going to church a decade earlier. I think that, like some Catholics of his generation, Dad felt as though the reforms of the Second Vatican Council did not go far enough and that the Church should be more welcoming. I also think that for someone of his intellectual and artistic sensibilities the ordinariness of parish life was challenging, despite his love of "the small things."

My desire to talk with him made me acknowledge my own hope—my own need—that maybe he could reconcile with the Church; maybe he would even consider going to confession one last time. In honestly reflecting on my own needs and desires, I also was confronting whether the real issue was that I wanted to feel as though I had done all I could to make death merciful for him—in a way that was actually most comfortable for me.

**

Though my father did spend some time at home initially, most of February 2013 was marked by hospital stays with brief respites at a nearby nursing home.

The last time I saw Dad, he was lying in bed at the nursing home—arguing about socks.

A couple of hours earlier, we had all been back in the apartment: Mom, Julia and I, and Bob. We were talking with a representative from a nursing organization that specialized in assisted-living arrangements. We wanted Dad to spend his last days at home.

It was Wednesday, and I could only stay for a couple of hours. I was planning to see Dad two days later, on Friday after my classes.

Then a frantic phone call came. "Dad's on the line," Mom shouted to us, "he needs socks, urgently."

One of the family secrets that had recently been revealed was that Dad was a compulsive sock hoarder. We had found pairs stashed all over the apartment.

So we rushed over to the nursing home and there we were—Mom, Julia, Bob, and I—standing around the bed, listening to Dad complain about the socks we had brought.

"Do, how can I wear these?" he said to my mother. "The wool's not right. They don't match."

"Oh now, Dick—I'm starting to get a little cross with you," Mom said gently.

I remember leaning against the windowsill, shaking my head, and muttering something like "tsk, tsk" under my breath, unsure about whether to express my frustration more openly.

Once he found the right pair, the conversation did turn to other things. Dad and Bob reminisced about my father as a nine-year-old choosing an especially valuable raffle prize: a Westclox wristwatch, which he immediately gave to Bob, saying, "There was nothing there that I wanted so I got this for you." The wristwatch was a little thing, but it symbolized a lifetime of brotherly love and affection. We also talked a little bit about the upcoming papal election, and dad mentioned that he thought I had performed well on television when I was recently interviewed about potential candidates.

It was getting late and we were long past visiting hours. I went to my dad's bed and kissed him on the forehead before leaving.

"I love you, Pops," I said.

"You know, I've always been proud of you," Dad said.

He spent Thursday evening with my mom, Julia, and Bob, but not with me—I was set for my visit Friday afternoon.

He passed away early Friday morning, February 22, 2013.

When I received the phone call from Mom and Bob giving me the news, my first response was anger: I should have been there, I would have been there. But that anger, I can honestly say, did pass quickly. Dad's last words to me were the words he wanted to be his last, I thought. In his own way, he was combining being a professor and a father—roles that had sometimes been complicated or confused during our lives together. And he was very much a professor and a father in those last days—as well as a husband, a brother, and a friend. It was a mercy that his death was without extended suffering, but the deeper mercy was that his death came in the presence of love.

***

I returned to the Infant Jesus Shrine in Bangalore about a year after Dad died. I went to the grotto to light a candle and make a donation, a thousand rupees this time, fifteen big ones. I then spent some time in prayer in the main chapel.

I gave thanks for the mercy of marriage—for the sacramental bond that gave my father and mother strength to face death.

I gave thanks for the mercy of honesty—my father's own honesty about his impending death which allowed me to be honest with myself about my own feelings and needs.

I gave thanks for the mercy of small things becoming big things—specifically Dad's idiosyncratic attachment to socks that gave me the opportunity to see him one last time and to hear the words that all sons long to hear.

I gave thanks for the mercy of family, for the reassuring presence of all of us, to Dad and to one another, during those last days.

I gave thanks that Dad did not experience extreme pain and suffering as he died—a physical mercy at the time of death.

I finally gave thanks for the mercy of the Church, a Church that welcomed back my father with a funeral Mass and a burial, each led by a gracious priest who understood the essence of my father as a teacher without even meeting him.

I had differences with my father. My father was a drinker; I was not, at least not anymore. My father did not want me to go into academics, but I chose to. My father expressed himself through images; I expressed myself through words.

As a family, we all had our differences with one another, too. As my father struggled with the disease itself, Julia, Mom, and I argued and disagreed about issues concerning treatment and care. We yelled, we cried.

But standing there, at the Infant Jesus Shrine, I realized that the memories of the differences that I had with my father—and that we all had with one another as a family—had moved mercifully into the background.

After my prayers of thanksgiving, I garlanded the Infant of Prague statue, as I had done the previous year. And I gently touched the statue's right foot.

I felt that Jesus hadn't been asking me for honor as a condition of His mercy. Instead, Jesus had asked me to reach out to Him for reassurance that His mercy would be there.

***

When I think about mercy and death now, the image that comes to mind is of Dad on his hospital bed in Maine. It's about a week after his diagnosis and he has returned to his room after one of the many intrusive tests that seem only to reconfirm what he and all of us already know about the seriousness of his condition.

Dad straightens himself to sit up in the bed. He looks at me and smiles.

"You know, Mathew, I've been thinking a lot about Jesus," he says.

I nod, indicating that I want to hear more.

"What Jesus did—it was all really simple; it was all about love."

Knowing Dad, I think he probably springboarded off of that declaration to expound on more abstract themes like time and consciousness or the beauty of small things.

Honestly, though, I don't remember what he said after that.

But I do remember realizing that my father had confided something personal to me in the way professors sometimes do—through a confident generalization that would probably sound better if delivered behind a lectern rather than from a hospital bed.

But I understood what Dad was really saying: he had experienced Jesus' love.

That was his opening to mercy, and it was enough for him. It was enough for us all.

Suggested Questions for Discussion

1. This story talks about experiencing mercy in the face of death. What particular mercies strike you as being most important?
2. When you think of mercy and death, what images come to mind?
3. Do you have an experience you could share when something small turned out to be something big, perhaps when a loved one died or was preparing for death?
4. How can the Church bring mercy into the experience of death and dying?

Suggested Questions for Private Reflection

1. If you still have unresolved differences with a loved one who has passed away, how could you look mercifully on those feelings?
2. How do you understand Jesus' love working through the process of death and dying?

Chapter Twelve

Mercy and Life

"I guess the worst thing you could do at that time was to have a beautiful baby," Caroline said after a few moments of silence.

"You shouldn't make any important life decisions before you contact her. Remember, she needs to be released too." Courtney was being confrontational, as always.

"I'm not so sure," I said.

We were talking about my adoption, and whether I should find my birthmother.

It was 1994 in Chicago, Illinois. I was newly sober and was attending my spiritual support group in a flat on the North Side, not far from Wrigley Field. There were about ten of us, sitting on chairs and couches that had been brought together in something resembling a circle. We all came with our own individual issues: doubt or depression; loneliness or marital problems; addiction or sexual abuse. What united us was an effort to see how we could reach out to God and to one another in a way that would give us strength and hope.

Courtney was one of the co-leaders of the group; she had a master's in psychology and was a practicing psychotherapist. She sat in a chair where the living room opened to the kitchen—she always had her legs propped up on an ottoman. Her body posture was relaxed, but her dark eyes were intense. It was difficult to withstand her gaze when she was making a point she felt you should acknowledge.

Will was the other co-leader—he was more soft-spoken and would usually ask questions in an almost-Socratic style, leading us to make connections between our feelings and our behavior that we would never had made on our own. Will was a highly regarded Catholic priest in the Chicago area and specialized in spiritual direction in academic contexts—he was recommended to me by a member of the faculty at the University of Chicago.

I owed my sobriety to Courtney and Will's confrontational approach. Although I never talked about my drinking with them until I actually got sober, their honesty and directness impacted me and brought me to a place where I could begin to confront my own issues. Now it was my adoption that had surfaced as the next issue I needed to face.

"Courtney's right about your birthmother," Will agreed. I think everyone else in the group nodded.

I felt like the circle was closing in on me.

But I held fast to my position. My parents, Carl and Dolores Schmalz, "Dick and Do," were my real parents. End of story. In any case, I added: "How do any of you know that my birthmother needs to be released from whatever—pain, guilt, her sense of responsibility? How do you know that she'd even be open to contact from me?"

"Mothers are mothers," Courtney said, looking me straight in the eye.

I don't remember whether the session ended there, or whether we moved on to another topic. But I do remember thinking that Courtney and Will were putting a heavy burden on me: I was supposed to bring mercy to my birthmother.

I wasn't sure that I needed—or was ready—to do that.

So, I ignored—I rejected—the challenge that Courtney and Will placed before me.

I ignored or rejected it for decades—until my adoption issue resurfaced in a way that showed me how messy mercy matters can be.

***

We all have our stories: not just "a" story, but "the" story—the story that defines who we are and where we come from. We add to the story over time, sometimes we change the characters, the plot, or even the moral. But there always is "the story" that explains or interprets all the other stories we tell.

There was never a time when I didn't know about my adoption. My parents told me everything they knew about the circumstances surrounding it. My birthparents were unmarried, and my birthmother was a college graduate who was considered to be particularly bright. In fact, she was a favorite among the nuns at the home for unwed mothers where she carried me to term. I never heard anything about my birthfather at all, and didn't know to what extent he was involved in the adoption process, or whether he knew about my birth at all.

After I was born, my birthmother receded into the background. My parents didn't know her name or anything about her career or family life afterward. Because the nuns wanted to place me in an academically inclined family, it took longer for me to actually be adopted, and I was taken care of by volunteers who came to the hospital over a period of four months.

More important to me than my birthparents were my parents—my real parents. I would never, and will never, use qualifications like "adoptive" or "foster." My parents Carl and Dolores Schmalz had a child, Stephen, who died of a brain tumor when he was twelve years old. It was after Stephen's death that I was adopted.

My parents told me that I could never be left alone when I was a baby—I would always cry so loudly. Many babies are like that, I know, but my fear of being alone persisted until a relatively late age. Up until middle school, I followed a ritual before bedtime. First, I would ask Dad to make the Sign of the Cross on my forehead and bless me. Then I would confirm where my mother would be in the house so that I would be sure that I could call or run to her if needed. Finally, I would always ask Grammy T—my mom's mom who lived with us for many years—to sit by my bed until I fell asleep. Every night Grammy T would faithfully pull up a chair and softly say her Rosary as I pulled the covers over my head and said my own prayers that my family would be kept safe throughout the night.

Being alone, being rejected. Those were my fears. None of that had to do with anything that my parents did or did not do. My family was loving and stable. But seemingly small things, like a bad grade or a disagreement with a friend, would bring tears. I was not beyond the occasional act of drama either. When I was rejected from Haverford College—my first-choice college—I stayed home from school for a full week. I felt as though I'd have been better off dead. And the prospect of death itself would bring its own deep fears, particularly that my parents would die and leave me and my sister, Julia, alone.

Those reactions and anxieties were not and are not unique to me or to adopted children. But for adopted children—for me—it's the intensity and often overwhelming power of such feelings that is difficult to describe, let alone to bear.

But that fear of being alone and rejected made my adoption stand out for me as a story of mercy: my birthmother chose life and my parents gave me a life—a wonderful life.

That's why I disagreed with Courtney and Will.

My story of adoption had taken its form as *the story* I was comfortable telling. I thought things were the way they were for a reason. I certainly did not believe that things could or would be better if I contacted my birthmother. Part of my resistance was the fear of being rejected. But another part of my resistance was an equally basic fear of change. Often the greatest mercy that an adopted child can receive is reassurance: reassurance that the fundamentals of life—family, friends, faith—will not or cannot change.

Boundaries can be barriers, but they also protect what we have. The boundary between my birthparents and my parents had been fixed ever since I could remember.

Sometimes the greatest mercy to others—and to oneself—is simply to let things be.

***

When I was contacted to write *Mercy Matters*, I felt it was a tall order. Even though I had been blogging for a decade, I wasn't sure whether my writing would be up to the challenge. But the greatest challenge, I thought, was taking seriously what I was writing about: that opening yourself to mercy is a life-changing gift.

I thought about Courtney and Will saying that my birthmother needed to be "released"—that she needed mercy. I didn't want to be writing a book on mercy and be a person who denied mercy to someone else who needed it.

That would be the worst kind of hypocrisy.

Courtney and Will's admonition that I release my birthmother echoed louder and louder in my conscience with each chapter of *Mercy Matters* that I wrote.

I had no way of knowing whether my birthmother felt as though she needed to be "released." And I was uncomfortable with the idea of finding out her name and contacting her out of the blue—though I had the legal right and means to do exactly that.

I heard horror stories of adopted children being rejected by their birthparents after making contact and how that contact irreparably damaged families by revealing secrets that no one was prepared for. But I also heard stories of adopted children finding heartfelt letters written to them by their birthparents at the time of adoption and over subsequent years. Those letters were mercies that led to understanding and acceptance and, in some cases, reconciliation.

Trying to quantify those two extremes and the intermediate variables, I worked out my calculus of mercy.

I would contact the original adoption agency and ask for non-identifying information about my birthparents as well as any correspondence left behind for me. If my birthmother and/or birthfather left anything that indicated that they would be open to contact with me, I would meet them halfway. And if either or both of them indicated they wanted "mercy" to release them from any guilt or shame that they felt, I was prepared to do or say whatever was necessary to set them free.

But if there were no correspondence for me, I wouldn't pursue the search. I would allow the boundary to remain and let things be.

***

I sent the letter requesting information and waited what seemed like a long time. A response from the adoption agency finally arrived.

The letter was kind—stating that the information might be overwhelming for me and that a social worker would be ready to support me if I wanted to continue my search. The letter made no mention of any correspondence for me and did not suggest that my birthparents wanted contact with me.

There was a record about the time of my birth, my length, and what I weighed. The letter also mentioned my initial IQ assessment and that I related well to others.

There was some information about my birthfather: he was twenty-eight years old, studying for a master's degree at the time of my adoption, and was good at woodworking.

But there was no information about my birthfather's ethnic or racial background, and no name. I didn't want a name anyway since I had requested non-identifying information.

There was much more information about my birthmother.

She was twenty-two years old and had graduated college by the time of my adoption. She was planning to be a teacher. She liked to knit and make clothes. There was an IQ assessment that, following standards used in the early 1960s, characterized her as "above average." She had no health issues except a rash that would appear on her face and arms when she became nervous. There was information about her ethnic and racial background.

And there also was a name: a first name. A very distinctive first name—not the kind you'd usually hear, even in the 1960s.

I didn't expect that.

I didn't think. I didn't pause to catch my breath.

I went right to my computer.

Given that unusual first name, the age, information about racial and ethnic identity, and with what I could surmise about the college she attended and her major, along with likely club or sorority interests, it didn't take me long. In fact, it only took me about fifteen minutes of searching the web and cross-referencing publicly available electronic databases, yearbooks, and newspaper stories.

I found an obituary.

The picture heading the obituary did not seem to bear a family resemblance at first, but Caroline said she saw me in the eyes. But all the information added up exactly: the first name, the age, the educational history, the ethnicity of the names on both the paternal and maternal sides, the Massachusetts background.

It had to be my birthmother.

But there was something else that sealed the connection for me. The obituary itself did not have much information about years and dates, but it did have a line about a study-abroad trip during the time my birthmother would have been pregnant with me. I took that as evidence that my birthmother had gone to great lengths to conceal my birth by accounting for that time frame in a very specific way. No other period of her over-seventy years of life was mentioned with that degree of exactness.

My birthmother had passed away about a year earlier, in a town not far from Worcester, where I have lived with my family for the last seventeen years. I found clips of the funeral on You-Tube.

Her longtime companion and her estranged husband—both too young to be my birthfather—preceded her in death.

The obituary also recorded that she had left two children, and a number of grandchildren.

I was the third child—but her firstborn. I had half-siblings, nieces, and nephews.

The recognition struck me, and the feelings finally came.

I felt sad; I felt guilty.

Most of all, I felt rejected—I was still a secret, still on the outside looking in.

***

"Help me make sense of this, Mom," I said.

I had called my mom in Virginia. She knew that I had tried to contact my birthparents and was totally supportive. She also had worked for the same agency that had facilitated my adoption and understood the legal and emotional issues involved. Several weeks earlier, I told my mom that I was almost certain that I had found my birthmother and that she had passed away.

"You have to know how things were back then, Mathew," Mom explained. "If you had a child out of wedlock, it was something you didn't want anyone to know about—not even your own parents. Women sometimes went to live with families who sponsored them. Most of the time they went to a home for unwed mothers. They knew the community would never accept them."

I knew that, but it was important to hear again, to understand what my birthmother had to overcome in carrying me to term: shame, guilt, ostracism. But I wanted to know why she evidently made no effort to contact me.

"Could she have left a letter?" I asked my mom.

"That was discouraged back then. But she did have you baptized. Her faith was important to her—you were important to her." I knew about my baptism. Catholicism was always part of "the story" of my adoption.

Mom continued, "But we did leave explicit permission at the adoption agency that we would have no objection if your birthmother wanted to contact you in the future."

"So, she could have contacted me?" I asked.

"Yes, she could have. But it would have been very, very difficult. She probably only would have known that we had given permission if she had taken the first step to contact the adoption agency. But any contact was discouraged during that time. We didn't ask for her name, she didn't ask for ours. That's the way things were. Everyone thought that it would make things easier."

A quick and immediate separation, a lifetime boundary, that's what went for mercy back in the early 1960s. Maybe it was merciful. I'm not sure. But the way adoption was set up, the entire responsibility fell on the birthmother. And I realized that I was doing the same thing: I had focused all this time on my birthmother, when my birthfather was equally responsible. But his was a responsibility that society didn't hold him to. He might have experienced guilt internally, but he didn't have to confront societal shame and ostracism.

I felt the need to reassure Mom: "You know, you and Dad were always my real parents. There never was an issue about belonging for me."

"Oh, sweetie, we always knew that," Mom said to me over the phone, and then repeated words that she had spoken to me countless times before: "You were always our beautiful baby boy."

***

Christopher David.

Those were the first and middle names—along with a very Irish-sounding surname.

I was—I had been—Christopher David. My birthmother's maiden name was—had been—my last name.

In Massachusetts, adopted children can request their pre-adoption birth certificate, and so I requested mine to finally confirm what I thought I knew.

Caroline handed me the unopened envelope when we were alone in the kitchen—I was just back from shopping and had set bags of vegetables and ready-made Indian food on the Formica floor by the refrigerator.

The envelope was manila and nondescript, except for the green certified-mail receipt. I opened the envelope and looked at the birth certificate, its black typescript standing out on a blue-and rose-colored paper that made me think of the sunset.

I took a breath and nodded to Caroline: the name of my birthmother matched that of the woman whose obituary I found.

"I guess the worst thing you could do at that time was to have a beautiful baby," Caroline said after a few moments of silence with all those shopping bags surrounding us.

She added, "I feel so sorry—so much sympathy—for her."

I went from the kitchen into the living room—feeling the pull of the smaller couch where I had struggled with my mercy day over the summer.

Veronica was nearby, on the big couch, writing up the results of her latest science experiment.

"I confirmed who my birthmother was, sweetie," I said.

"Okay," Veronica replied, not breaking her focus on tabulating the effects of artificial sweeteners on flatworms.

I lay there on the couch for a couple of minutes with my eyes closed—thinking that I really requested the birth certificate because I hoped that I was wrong, not because I wanted to be right.

"Honey, can you go out to receive Joy since you still have your coat on?" Caroline's voice broke the silence, and I opened my eyes. I realized that I hadn't removed my blue parka or taken off my running shoes.

I sprung up from the couch and went out to get Joy who had

just been dropped off by the school bus.

"We're going to get your new tennis clothes today, honey," I said when we met in the middle of our ice-covered driveway.

"Thank you, Daddy! Can you carry my backpack? It's so heavy, and I don't want to slip."

With the backpack hanging on my shoulder, I held on to Joy as we skated up the driveway together, aiming for the garage door so we could enter our house via the basement.

I blurted out: "I found my birthmother, honey. It was who we thought it was."

Joy stopped on the ice like a hockey player who realized the flow of the game had shifted.

"The husband! Who was the husband?" she asked excitedly.

"There was no husband—no father's name was listed," I said. On my birth certificate there were only horizontal dashes and empty spaces in the box for "father." No name, no information of any kind, was recorded.

"Aw—but I still have cousins, right?" Joy said as we made it safely into the garage.

"Yes, you do," I said, feeling the ache of responsibility with each and every word.

There wasn't—there isn't—room to feel anything else.

***

Would it be a mercy to contact my half-siblings and their families? Or would the mercy be to leave things as they are?

Caroline, Veronica, and Joy are comfortable with me answering those questions as I see fit.

But the questions aren't about what would be most merciful for me; they're questions about what would be most merciful for us all as a family—an extended family defined and separated by a long-held secret.

Revealing secrets can be liberating—but it can also be shattering.

Back in Chicago over two decades ago, Courtney and Will

were sure that revealing the secret would be a mercy to both me and my birthmother. But I think now, as I did back then, that charging someone else with "being merciful" in a specific way is something that very few people have the knowledge or insight to do. If we want to help someone to believe in mercy's transformative power, it's far better to share our own experiences in an honest and loving way than it is to make a snap judgment of what will necessarily be right or appropriate for another person.

In the end, being open to mercy—giving it, receiving it, asking for it—is something that relates most intimately to the relationship we have with God and how we discern His love for all of us.

So, for now, I will do the only thing that I can do: bring my questions to the "throne of grace" and ask for mercy and grace to help in my time of need (see Heb 4:16).

My adoption story hasn't concluded yet, and perhaps it will never conclude in some sort of neat, easily explainable way. As *the story* that explains the other stories I tell, the narrative may very well have new plot lines and twists, along with different characters coming into view. But regardless of what happens or does not happen, for me my adoption story will continue to be a story of mercy, of love that responds to the human need for love—a story about choosing life, and all that comes with it.

Choosing life is always messy.

But it is there in the messiness, in the conflicted and often confused ways we live our lives, that we can learn how much mercy matters to us all.

Suggested Questions for Discussion

1. What is your reaction to the story? What issues does it raise for you?
2. Would you characterize the approach to adoption in the 1960s as merciful?

3. How can we be merciful to all those involved in adoption (adopted children, birthparents, adoptive parents, siblings)?

4. What do you think about the decision facing the author? How would you approach it?

Suggested Questions for Private Reflection

1. What's "the story" for you that explains all the other stories you tell?

2. In what ways is your life "messy" and in need of mercy?

LIST OF PSEUDONYMS

Chapter One
Joyce Richardson; Stan

Chapter Two
Zach

Chapter Three
Caroline; Joy; Veronica

Chapter Four
Caroline; Father Thompson; St. Agatho

Chapter Five
Father Khrist Bhakt; Father Prem Annand; Father Sanchit

Chapter Six
Aimée; Brigitte; Carrie; Cristi; Joy; Maria; Margo; Mr. Prakash; Rob; Sharmila

Chapter Seven
Dieter; Esther; Vicky

Chapter Eight
Anthony; Diego; Father Ed; Francis; Graced Opportunities; Luis; Pablo; Ricky; Roger

Chapter Nine
Annette; Connor; Ellen; Rachel; Sarah

Chapter Eleven
Caroline

Chapter Twelve
Caroline; Courtney; Joy; Veronica; Will

ENDNOTES

Introduction

[1] The official website for the Jubilee of Mercy can be found at http://www.im.va/content/gdm/en.html.

[2] Inés San Martín, "Everything You Need to Know About the Holy Year of Mercy," *Crux: Covering All Things Catholic*, December 7, 2015, http://www.cruxnow.com/church/2015/12/07/everything-you-need-to-know-about-the-holy-year-of-mercy/.

[3] Inés San Martín, "Opening the Holy Year, Francis Says Mercy Always Trumps Judgment," *Crux: Covering All Things Catholic*, December 8, 2015, http://www.cruxnow.com/church/2015/12/08/opening-the-holy-year-francis-says-mercy-always-trumps-judgment/.

[4] Ibid.

[5] Pope Francis, *Misericordiae Vultus*, Bull of Indiction of the Extraordinary Jubilee of Mercy, April 11, 2015.

[6] *Misericordiae Vultus*, 1.

[7] *Misericordiae Vultus*, 2.

[8] *Misericordiae Vultus*, 7.

[9] *Misericordiae Vultus*, 8.

[10] *Misericordiae Vultus*, 9.

[11] Ibid.

[12] *Misericordiae Vultus*, 6.

[13] *Misericordiae Vultus*, 15.

[14] Ibid.

[15] *Misericordiae Vultus*, 12.

[16] *Misericordiae Vultus*, 20.

[17] Ibid.

[18] *Misericordiae Vultus*, 14.

Chapter One

[1] St. Augustine, *Confessions*, trans. Henry Chadwick, (Oxford: Oxford University Press, 1991), IX.viii.18,168.

[2] Ibid.

Chapter Two

[1] This essay draws upon material first published on the website On Faith (http://www.faithstreet.com/onfaith). See Mathew N. Schmalz, "Before Easter: An Essential Penance," *On Faith*, April 15, 2011, http://www.faithstreet.com/onfaith/2011/04/15/before-easter-an-essential-penance/35762.

[2] Anonymous (2011-03-30). *Baltimore Catechism, No. 1* (19-20). Kindle Edition.

Chapter Five

[1] I have written about Ghura Paul extensively in scholarly publications. This chapter draws upon general details of his life as discussed in those publications, but addresses my personal relationship with him in a way that I have not written about previously. Relevant publications that discuss Ghura Paul include: Mathew N. Schmalz, "Materialities of Jesus in North India," *Material Religion in South Asia*, eds. Tracy Pitchman and Corinne G. Dempsey (Albany: SUNY Press, 2015), 67-88; Mathew N. Schmalz, "Thinking Through and Staying With," *Engaging South Asian Religions: Boundaries, Appropriations and Resistances*, eds. Mathew N. Schmalz and Peter Gottschalk (Albany: SUNY Press, 2011), 233-234; Mathew N. Schmalz, "Dalit Catholic Tactics of Marginality at a North Indian Mission," *History of Religions* 44 (February 2005): 216-251; Mathew N. Schmalz, "Images of the Body in the Life and Death of a North Indian Catholic Catechist," *History of Religions* 39 (November 1999): 177-201.

² I also discuss this scene in Schmalz (1999), 177-78; another account of the scene appears in a magazine put out by the charismatic prayer center, see Sri Ghura Paul, "*Vah Tejab jo Atma ko Jala na Saki*," ["The Acid that Could Not Burn the Soul"] *Vacan Sudha* (Varanasi: Divine Printers, 1995), 10.

³ For a full discussion of the theories surrounding the attack, see Schmalz (1999), 181-87.

⁴ I also discuss this song and the circumstances surrounding it in my dissertation, see Mathew N. Schmalz, *A Space for Redemption: Catholic Tactics in Hindu North India* (University of Chicago, Ph.D. diss.), 267,273.

Chapter Six

¹ An initial version of this chapter was published on the website Crux: Covering All Things Catholic (http://www.cruxnow.com). See Mathew N. Schmalz, "Touching and Being Touched at Sumanahalli," Crux: Covering All Things Catholic, September 1, 2015, http://www.cruxnow.com/faith/2015/08/31/touching-and-being-touched-at-sumana-halli/.

² The song's Hindi title is "*Yeh Shaam Mastanani*" and can be found on YouTube, https://www.youtube.com/watch?v=_sZg4EUB3IM.

³ The website for Sumanahalli can be found at http://www.sumanahalli.net/.

⁴ This quotation was provided to me in a PowerPoint presentation sent by Sumanahalli's Director, Father Peter D'Souza. The quotation is also referenced at http://www.claret.org/en/mission-alive/sumanahalli-social-hub-bangalore.

⁵ John Paul II, *Evangelium Vitae* (March 25, 1995), 34, http://w2.vatican.va/content/john-paul-ii/en/encyclicals/documents/hf_jp-ii_enc_25031995_evangelium-vitae.html.

⁶ Ibid., 35.

⁷ Anonymous, *Anima Christi*, http://www.preces-latinae.org/thesaurus/PostMissam/AnimaChristi.html.

Chapter Eight

¹ See St. Thérèse of Lisieux, *Story of a Soul The Autobiography of St. Thérèse of Lisieux*, trans. John Clarke, O.C.D. (Washington: ICS Publications, 1996). (Kindle Location, 734).

² Dorothy Day, *The Long Loneliness: An Autobiography* (San Francisco: Harper San Francisco, 1952), 285.

Chapter Nine

¹ This chapter draws extensively upon two previously published pieces: Mathew N. Schmalz, "Where Do We Put Tamerlan Tsarnaev?" On Faith, May 6, 2013, http://www.faithstreet.com/onfaith/2013/05/06/where-do-we-put-tamerlan-tsarnaev/10015; Mathew N. Schmalz, "Should We Forgive the Boston Marathon Bomber," Crux: Covering All Things Catholic, January 5, 2015, http://www.cruxnow.com/faith/2015/01/05/should-we-forgive-dzhokhar-tsarnaev/.

² Diane Williamson, "Misguided Outrage on Main St.," Worcester Telegram and Gazette, May 5, 2013, http://www.telegram.com/article/20130505/COLUMN01/105059772/1101/local.

³ Denise LaVoie, "Uncle Arranging Boston Bomb Suspect's Burial Rites," Associated Press, May 5, 2013, http://news.yahoo.com/uncle-arranging-boston-bomb-suspects-burial-rites-163554313.html.

⁴ Ibid.

⁵ Ibid.

6   Greg Botelho and Paula Newton, "To Locals' Surprise, Ta-merlan Tsarnaev Buried in Virginia Cemetery," CNN, May 11, 2013, http://www.cnn.com/2013/05/10/us/virginia-boston-suspect-burial/.

7   Ibid.

8   Ibid.

9   Yvonne Abraham, "Charlie Baker Takes the Proust Question-naire," *Boston Globe*, October 15, 2014, https://www.boston-globe.com/metro/2014/10/15/charlie-baker-takes-proust-questionnaire/p2B2GsYFIUnYnVLsZCiX3I/story.html.

10 Massachusetts Catholic Conference, "A Statement of the Roman Catholic Bishops of Massachusetts on the Death Penalty" (April 7, 2015), http://www.macatholic.org/sites/macatholic.org/files/assets/Statement%20on%20the%20Death%20Penalty%204.7.2015.pdf%20FINAL.pdf.

11 Ibid.

12 Ibid.

13 "Read Boston Bomber Tsarnaev's Full Statement," *Time* magazine, June 24, 2015, http://time.com/3934592/boston-bomber-dzhokhar-tsarnaev-apology/.

14 Ibid.

15 Ibid.

16 "Boston Victims Condemn Bomber's Insincere Apology," *Daily Mail*, June 24, 2015, http://www.dailymail.co.uk/news/article-3137550/Boston-bombing-survivors-arrive-court-face-Dzhokhar-Tsarnaev-formally-sentenced-death.html.

17 Ibid.

18 Hilary Sargent and Dialynn Dwyer, "Tsarnaev Moved to Supermax Prison: Here's How He'll Live," Boston.com, July 17, 2015, http://www.boston.com/news/local/2015/07/17/tsarnaev-moved-supermax-prison-here-how-live/pgzDWN-rA8zk4bX7qhuSL0L/story.html.

19 "Boston Victims Condemn Bomber's Insincere Apology,"
    Daily Mail.
20 Ibid.
21 Ibid.

Chapter Ten

1   This chapter reproduces much of a previously published
    piece: Mathew N. Schmalz, "The Abyss of Mercy," Crux:
    Covering All Things Catholic, April 10, 2015, http://www.
    cruxnow.com/faith/2015/04/10/the-abyss-of-mercy/.
2   For a full discussion of the trip to Madhu, see Mathew N.
    Schmalz, "A Pilgrimage to Madhu," *America*, January 9,
    2015, http://americamagazine.org/pilgrimage-madhu.
3   Cardinal Walter Kasper, *Mercy: The Essence of the Gospel and
    the Key to Christian Li*fe (Mahwah, NJ: Paulist Press, 2013),
    Kindle Edition.
4   Ibid. (Kindle Locations, 537-38).
5   Daniel P. Moloney, "What Mercy Is," *First Things*, March
    2015, http://www.firstthings.com/article/2015/03/what-
    mercy-is.
6   Ibid.
7   Kasper (Kindle Location, 1744).
8   Ibid. (Kindle Location, 3416).
9   Ibid. (Kindle Location, 2746).
10 Maria Faustina Kowalska, *Diary of Saint Maria Faustina
    Kowalska*, (Stockbridge, MA: Marian Press, 2014) (Kindle
    Location, 12041).
11 Ibid. (Kindle Locations, 2105-06).
12 Pope Francis, *Evangelii Gaudium* (November 24, 2103), 3,
    http://w2.vatican.va/content/francesco/en/apost_exhorta-
    tions/documents/papa-francesco_esortazione-ap_20131124_
    evangelii-gaudium.html.
13 Kowalska (Kindle Location, 1106).

14   Ibid., (Kindle Location, 2241).

Chapter Eleven

1   For a virtual "tour" of the Infant Jesus Shrine, see http://
     www.catholicsandcultures.org/india/shrines-pilgrimage/
     miraculous-infant-jesus-church.
2   Paul Blanshard, *American Freedom and Catholic Power* (Bos-
     ton: Beacon Press, 1949).
3   Pope Francis references Teilhard de Chardin in section III.83
     of *Laudato Si'*, see Pope Francis, *Laudato Sí* (May 24, 2015),
     http://w2.vatican.va/content/francesco/en/encyclicals/docu-
     ments/papa-francesco_20150524_enciclica-laudato-si.html.